THE *SAVVY* GUIDE
TO CAR MAINTENANCE
AND REPAIR

WITHDRAWN
FROM THE RECORDS OF THE
MID-CONTINENT PUBLIC LIBRARY

629.28722 C386   SEP   2006
Chase, Kate.
The savvy guide to car
 maintenance and repair

MID-CONTINENT PUBLIC LIBRARY
Parkville Branch
8815 N.W. 45 Highway
Parkville, MO 64152   **PV**

Other books in the *SAVVY* Guide series

The Savvy Guide to Home Theater, ISBN 0-7906-1303-4
The Savvy Guide to Digital Photography, ISBN 0-7906-1309-3
The Savvy Guide to Fantasy Sports, ISBN 0-7906-1313-1
The Savvy Guide to Home Security, ISBN 0-7906-1315-8
The Savvy Guide to Digital Music, ISBN 0-7906-1317-4
The Savvy Guide to Motorcycles, ISBN 0-7906-1316-6

THE *SAVVY* GUIDE
TO CAR MAINTENANCE
AND REPAIR

KATE J. CHASE

INDY-TECH PUBLISHING

Indianapolis

MID-CONTINENT PUBLIC LIBRARY
Parkville Branch
8815 N.W. 45 Highway
Parkville, MO 64152

PV

MID-CONTINENT PUBLIC LIBRARY - QU

3 0003 00045917 0

© 2006 by Sams Technical Publishing, LLC, under the Indy-Tech Publishing imprint.
Indy-Tech Publishing is an imprint of Sams Technical Publishing, LLC, 9850 E. 30th St., Indianapolis IN 46229.

All rights reserved. No part of this book shall be reproduced, stored in a retrieval system, or transmitted by any means, electronic, mechanical, photocopying, recording or otherwise, without written permission from the publisher. No patent liability is assumed with respect to the use of the information contained within. While every precaution has been taken in the preparation of this book, the author, the publisher, or seller assumes no responsibility for errors and omissions. Neither is any liability assumed for damages or injuries resulting from the use of information contained herein. The advice and strategies contained within may not be suitable for every situation. This book is sold with the understanding that the publisher is not engaged in rendering legal, accounting or other professional services. The fact that an organization or website is referred to in this work as a citation or potential source of further information does not mean that the author or the publisher endorses the information the organization or website may provide or recommendations a third party may make. Please be aware that websites referenced in this text may have changed or disappeared between the time the book was written and the time at which you read it.

As this book may be technical in nature, we recommend that a professional be consulted if you feel you have gone too far.

International Standard Book Number: 0-7906-1321-2

Chief Executive Officer:	Alan Symons
President:	Scott Weaver
Chief Financial Officer:	Keith Siergiej
Chief Operating Officer:	Richard White
Acquisitions Editor:	Brad Schepp
Editorial Assistant:	Dana Eaton
Copy Editor:	Cheryl Hoffman
Typesetter:	Cheryl Hoffman
Cover Design:	Robin Roberts and Mike Walsh
Interior Illustrations:	Provided by the author unless otherwise noted
Interior Photos:	Provided by the author unless otherwise noted
Drawings:	Provided by the author unless otherwise noted

Trademark acknowledgments: Where the names of companies, brands, etc are used, the registered trademarks have generally been noted. The companies mentioned in this text in no way endorse the contents of this book, nor have they participated in the publication of this book. All product illustrations, name and logos are trademarks of their respective manufacturers, including all terms in this book that are known or suspected to be trademarks or service marks. Use of an illustration, term, or logo in this book should not be regarded as affecting the validity of any trademark or service mark, or regarded as an association with or endorsement from the respective trademark holder.

Manufactured in the USA.

CONTENTS

1 GETTING COMFORTABLE WITH YOUR VEHICLE

- ◆ Reviewing your owner's manual

- ◆ Using your vehicle manufacturer's Web site

- ◆ Learning from the pros

- ◆ Finding and taking advantage of a good auto parts store

- ◆ Identifying basic issues about the computer in your vehicle

- ◆ Knowing your vehicle's warranty details

- ◆ Keeping your own record

The first step in working with your vehicle is simply to know more about it: the features, the kind of maintenance your make and model demands, and where you can find additional information to help you in your work.

Considering we're the people who spend the most time with our vehicles—that is, besides the "quality" time our wheels spend parked in a garage, driveway, parking lot, or on the street—it only seems appropriate that we should know them best. Indeed, we usually know what sounds and feels "normal" because we grow familiar with how they operate and respond.

Yet the reality is that we often don't know a lot about our vehicles beyond what we experience directly. While there are people who really look beneath the hood before they buy, they're probably in the minority. And there may be even less incentive to peer beneath the hood once we've gotten that new purchase home.

It's when a problem hits that you can instantly feel transformed into a stranger in a strange and unwelcoming land. The more serious the problem, whether it's a sudden and troublesome noise or that the darned thing won't start, the greater that sense of unfamiliarity. You pop the hood, look within, and feel like you're lost.

So this first chapter is all about helping you get comfortable and familiar with your vehicle without being a mechanic. Once you have a basic sense of how things are supposed to look and run and connect, it's going to become much easier to spot when something is off kilter. You'll get a bonus here, too: a certain sense of confidence and control over this great beast you depend upon to get you where you want to go.

REVIEWING YOUR OWNER'S MANUAL

Way too many of us only look at our owner's manuals twice: once when we buy the vehicle and again when we're cleaning out the glove compartment because we're about to sell the car or trade it in. This is a real shame when you stop to consider how much information can be found in the booklet.

While few of us are going to find the manual a great read, it's well worth your time to sit down with it and see what is there. A good owner's manual usually includes the following:

- Specific details about your model such as standard and special features
- General warranty information and coverage
- Proper maintenance techniques and recommendations for frequency and type (such as for antifreeze, oil, and other fluids)
- Part numbers and/or types for frequently replaced parts such as headlights, bulbs, and fuses, as well as tire type and size
- Warnings ("only use this type, not that type")
- An area to record your maintenance and service information such as when you need to change the oil

Going through Your Vehicle Using the Manual as a Guide

Once you've reviewed your owner's manual, it makes sense to use the manual as a guide to identify the parts of your car. Many manuals will actually diagram what you're looking at when you

Savvy Tip

You wouldn't believe how many people don't even know how to pop the hood on their vehicles. That's something you don't want to learn how to do while you're stuck along the side of a dark road with little light available to you. So check your owner's manual to see how to open the hood and make sure you can get inside.

pop the hood, so you can identify parts like the carburetor, the air filter, the oil stick, and the radiator, and find out how you can check your brake fluid and automatic transmission fluid levels.

When you're finished beneath the hood, go through other areas like the tires, the trunk, and beneath the dashboard while continuing to follow the diagrams in your owner's manual until you feel you have a sense of what's what.

Doing It Now Rather than Later

Understand that the best time to review what's under your hood is before you have a problem. If you see how the setup appears when everything is working well, it's going to be much easier for you to spot things like a disconnected hose, a dangling wire, or a loose battery cable.

I've purchased two new cars where not every part under the hood was connected. It took some detective work to determine that, in one case, one wire was not meant to be connected under normal circumstances, and that in the second, the car managed to leave the factory without the connection having been made. This is far easier to spot check on a new vehicle than under the hood of a hard-used and poorly maintained car or truck. If I'd waited to look until a problem with the vehicle developed, I might have been left wondering.

Do you have questions about what you see? If your vehicle is new, or relatively new, or under warranty, schedule a time to take your vehicle into the dealer and have an experienced service representative go through your vehicle with you to help you identify parts and answer any questions you may have. This one step can save you a bundle in time and worry later on because it further reduces the mystery of how your vehicle works and how different parts connect.

Compatible Replacement Parts

You'll quickly discover that your owner's manual specifies exact part numbers that are usually made or authorized by the manufacturer. However, you may pay slightly to a great deal more if you only buy from the manufacturer or its parts centers.

There are many automotive parts manufacturers that offer compatible hardware. Bulbs, fuses, and headlights are a perfect example of this. The last time I went to my dealer to get a replacement headlamp for my car, the cost was more than $58. Ouch! But when I went to my local auto parts store equipped with the replacement part number from my owner's manual, I was able to find a compatible headlamp from another parts manufacturer for under $20. That left me with nearly $40 that I could spend on other parts I needed.

You can use this technique too. Look up the part information in your owner's manual and jot this information down. Then go to your auto parts store and look for a compatible replacement based on the manufacturer's replacement details.

Supplementary Books

Did you know that you can buy a whole book devoted just to the subject of your vehicle (or one manufactured virtually identically)? Many publishers produce books specific to a make and model or that cover similar makes and models (e.g.,Toyota Tercel Service Manual, 1980-88 models). These publishers include the well-known Chilton, Haynes, and Clymer.

These books are a big step up from the owner's manual because they often diagram all major components for you, like the Haynes manual for my Suzuki Sidekick shown in figure 1-1. They're also not quite as marketing or public relations–oriented as an owner's manual and are usually written by people who know a particular model inside out. These make important additions to your car repair and maintenance tool kit and often pay for themselves the first time or two you use them.

Fig. 1-1: This supplemental book covering a particular make and model of vehicle includes advanced diagrams.

If you want to take the book out with you to make repairs or perform maintenance (a smart step), consider getting a clear Lucite or plastic cover or sleeve so you don't get the book marked up with grease and dirt. A transparent plastic bag of the right size can be pressed into service as a temporary book sleeve.

Just about the very first thing I do when I get a new (at least to me) vehicle on which I plan to do regular small repairs and maintenance is to find at least one good book written specifically about that make and model. About ten years ago, when faced with a 1988 Suzuki Samurai that was having some serious oil-burning problems, I just couldn't afford to pop a new engine into the darned thing. Instead, my partner and I invested in a supplemental book specifically for this model that showed us exactly how the engine is laid out so we could literally take the engine apart and make a repair deep within. Without the book, we couldn't have done it and gotten an extra year out of the vehicle before we finally bought a refurbished engine to replace the old one.

If you don't have a lot of money, you may be able to find these books at your local library or through interlibrary loan (ask your librarian how you can check). You might also explore used bookstores in your area or go online with one of the big Internet bookstores like Amazon.com, Overstock.com, Half.com, or Barnes and Noble (www.bn.com) to see if you can order a discounted new copy or a used copy. Even brand new, these copies rarely cost more than $18 to $25.

For best results, read through a section before you take the book out to the vehicle. It's just harder to "get" everything when you're reading for the first time while also looking through the vehicle.

USING YOUR CAR MANUFACTURER'S WEB SITE

Unlike sites offered by the makers of computers or consumer electronics, car manufacturers' Web sites often are devoted primarily to getting you to buy the new model; they often aren't

Can't find what you need at a manufacturer's Web site? Try using the Search feature to look or explore the site map, which lists the major topics covered by the site.

Savvy Tip

As you familiarize yourself with online resources to keep your vehicle in good running shape, don't forget to check out the message boards or Web discussion boards you find online. Such places tend to be popular with enthusiastic hobbyists, serious car techs, and people like you who have learned their way around a bumper and radiator. Post a question on these boards and you may get anywhere from one or two to a slew of responses you can print out and review.

great repositories of detailed information that can help you out of a jam. In fact, many just lead you to a dealer or authorized service center in your area.

But Web sites change over time and not all car manufacturers' sites exclude really useful information. Some allow you to order a missing owner's manual (and let's face it—almost all of us have bought a used car that's missing this important booklet) or locate specific parts or accessories. So find out the Web site address (called a URL, or universal resource locator) for your manufacturer, then visit and explore deeply to see what is there. Most manufacturers are pretty easy to find. For example, Toyota can be found at www.toyota.com; Ford at www.ford.com; and Volvo at www.volvocars.com

Often, it's helpful to look under the Parts and Service link found on many of the sites . It's possible you'll just be directed to a dealer, but it's always worth a try. If you can't locate the Web site address for your vehicle maker, use a big Web search engine such as Google at www.google .com or Dogpile at www.dogpile.com.

LEARNING FROM THE PROS

One of the fastest ways to benefit from the knowledge and helpfulness of car repair pros—outside of being lucky enough to live next door to the world's best mechanic—is to go online. If you often use the Web (and let's face it, the Internet is like the world's biggest library) for research, you may already be aware of how many home improvement as well as do-it-yourself auto repair sites are available. If you don't, are you ever going to be pleasantly surprised!

Appendix A offers you a compendium of some very helpful Web sites (of the sort shown in figure 1-2) that can help you find out more about your specific vehicle, learn more about how a particular system on your vehicle operates (e.g., transmission, fuel injection, heating and cooling, exhaust), and how to perform additional repairs beyond what you'll read here.

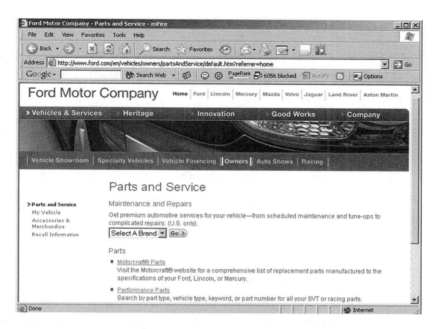

Fig. 1-2: An example (www.ford.com) of the many helpful Web sites that explain basic auto repairs and help you understand what you're working with.

It's smart always to consult more than one online resource when you're looking for details. Different professionals posting information online may offer conflicting advice or quite different techniques for solving a problem. Just as it's wise to get a second—or third—opinion when the issue is your health, the same holds true for your vehicle's health and operation. You may also discover that you feel comfortable trying one technique while another seems waaaay too complicated.

Finally, understand that not everyone who calls himself or herself a pro really is. Or the pro may be very experienced with one type of vehicle but not with another. So read and research before you jump into something.

Your phone book's yellow pages will give you a listing of auto parts stores, usually under Automotive Parts or Car Parts and Repair. But if you happen to know "average Joes" who do a lot of their own repairs, ask them which store(s) they use. It's a good bet such folks have taken the time to learn which stores offer decent pricing as well as good inventory and resources.

Know the hours of your regular auto parts stores; some open very early but also close up shop relatively early, like 5 p.m. Big chain stores are frequently open longer hours. Also identify those that are open on Sunday (not all are).

You can find pros in real life, too. A good garage is a great place to start. But even if you want to go the do-it-yourself route, you have some avenues to explore. One good example can be found in many auto parts stores where the employees may be retired mechanics or simply very knowledgeable about vehicles and how they work. Let's look at them next.

FINDING AND TAKING ADVANTAGE OF A GOOD AUTO PARTS STORE

Don't think of an auto parts store as just a place to buy new wiper blades or find an odd fuse or light bulb. Most of them offer far more than that. It's the extras that make them a better choice for buying your parts than a huge discount general merchandise store. While you won't always find an experienced auto technician manning the counter at an auto parts store, that's often the case. Beyond that, many of the folks working there are apt to be fairly knowledgeable about auto repair. And where their knowledge ends, they frequently have access to books, computer software, and other resources that can really help you.

I recommend that anyone who's serious about trying to perform some of his or her own repairs and maintenance—and that includes you, right?—spend a little time getting familiar with local auto parts stores. It's best to do this when you have the time to poke around the store and ask questions rather than in the heat of an emergency.

When you're checking out an auto parts store, listen to the conversations going on inside. Seek out clerks who seem especially knowledgeable and ask them questions. For example, you may want to

- tell them what kind of vehicle(s) you're working with and ask how well stocked the store is in parts for that model;
- ask what resources they have for looking up the parts you'll need;
- when you're trying to avoid costly manufacturer-specific items, ask what alternative brands the clerks recommend and/or use for their own vehicles; and
- mention a specific problem you're having and see if they offer advice or recommendations for troubleshooting and repair.

HELP AND SERVICE PERSONIFIED

Walk into a good auto parts shop when a mechanic from a local garage happens to be there picking up parts and you'll often overhear the mechanic and store clerk brainstorming a problem. If mechanics get extra help there, so can you.

You'll discover that some stores go way beyond just selling parts: and are happy to share their knowledge. If you happen to bring the troubled vehicle along with you, don't be too surprised if a clerk or technician offers to go out and eyeball your vehicle or show you how to install a part. Sometimes a clerk will even roll up his or her sleeves to help you install a new battery or offer to run an easy diagnostic test for you.

It's because so many shops have helpful personnel that I recommend you shop around to find a good auto parts store and give it your repeat business. It's not too hard to find one that features decent prices and a high level of service and experience.

Many shops realize how many non-pros, including women, are doing their own repair and maintenance to reduce costs. To stay competitive, they provide extra resources to help you and earn your repeat business. In fact, many women interviewed for this book reported that auto parts store staff members went out with them to the parking lot to show them exactly what to do or simply did the job for them while they watched. Yet most of these stores only charge you for the parts you buy and not for the extra service they provide. Today, that's a real deal. But rather than just depending on finding the right staff member to save the day, knowledgeable do-it-yourselfers use it as a learning experience so they can tackle the job themselves the next time around.

I think almost all of us have been in the big chain auto stores where they have acres full of just about every part, accessory, and tool imaginable. But have you ever visited one of those old-time auto parts stores and felt like you'd crossed into a strange and different land? The people there seem to talk a foreign language and can cite long and complicated parts numbers and descriptions without referring to a single book.

But don't be put off by such a place just because it may not seem as clean, organized, or well-stocked as a big-name chain store in the local strip mall or shopping center. Such old-line stores can be a repository of people with many years of experience working both with garages and consumers. They also may stock both common and more exotic parts as well as ones that fall between vehicle maintenance/repair and general hardware categories. The pros behind the counter are usually quite eager to assist you, and if they don't have a part, they probably can get it pretty quickly, often within one or two days (though they may require a deposit to be sure they don't order it only to have you go and buy it elsewhere). In other words, these nonchain stores can be precious gems.

Understanding the Computer in Your Car

One thing many people fail to realize is that our vehicles—just like our offices—have become largely computerized. Sure, we might still have a carburetor and other familiar parts, but since the 1980s, most vehicles have been equipped with an engine that is largely controlled by an onboard computer surprisingly similar to the PC on your desktop at work or home. Too often, the onboard computer isn't very well documented in the owner's manual (and I've seen more than a few that didn't discuss the computer at all).

The computer does a lot of different jobs, including the following:

- Storing details about your vehicle in its basic input/output system (BIOS) just as your desktop PC keeps track of the date and time and what hardware is connected. A car's BIOS, for example, often stores the Vehicle Identification Number (VIN), the unique alphanumeric ID assigned to every car, truck, and SUV.
- Making adjustments as needed to keep the vehicle's performance up to snuff (e.g., if the fuel-air mix is a little off, the computer tweaks the system to try to make the vehicle run better).
- Keeping track of problems it detects and generating a Diagnostic Trouble Code (DTC) to help a mechanic or a savvy owner identify what's wrong.

As you'll discover as we work together in this book, that computer also has some powerful control over your vehicle. For example, the computer can literally disable your vehicle if it detects a problem it can no longer tweak or correct. This situation can be at least as frustrating as when your parents took away your keys as punishment—or worse, because it's hard to appeal to the computer to relent and let you go on your way.

However, what you need to understand right now is that the computer won't flash a message on your dashboard telling you, "Hey! You've got a loose fan belt." Instead, it's going to generate a code. Once you get that code, you have to look up what it means. Many cars' owner's manuals today provide listings of the most common codes so check there first. You also may be able

Can't locate a copy of your warranty? Contact the dealer where you purchased your vehicle and ask for it. Most dealers are very helpful in providing warranty copies.

to obtain an explanation of these codes from the manufacturer's Web site or from your local service dealer, auto parts store, or garage.

In chapter 2 you'll learn how to communicate with your onboard computer to decode its mysteries using special diagnostic tools you can buy at your local auto parts store or shop for online.

KNOWING YOUR VEHICLE'S WARRANTY DETAILS

Is your vehicle still under warranty? If so, you want to be careful that you don't do anything that invalidates that warranty. If you do, you could end up wasting money by losing the remaining period of coverage left on your vehicle.

While most manufacturers won't invalidate a warranty over something simple (e.g., you replaced their fuse with something compatible made by a different manufacturer), they can get very fussy if you have a major system like the transmission, fuel injectors, or drive train worked on by a nonauthorized garage and then return to the authorized center for additional help. This is also true if you try to do major repairs yourself.

You want to really examine your warranty and see what it spells out. Look specifically for what the plan covers and what you have to pay out of your own pocket. Once you've reviewed your warranty, make an educated decision about how to proceed. Most of the repairs we'll discuss here aren't going to get you into trouble with your warranty. But if you need a major repair, you need to choose carefully whether to take it to your local all-purpose repair shop or head for the authorized service center.

But let's be realistic. Not all of us make full use of our warranties. While some people choose to faithfully return their car or truck to an authorized service center for every little thing, many of us don't, either because we're not crazy about the service or because we have to wait too long for an appointment or just because the nearest authorized service center is located quite a distance from our homes. If you're not going to use your warranty, then you're under fewer restrictions. But be sure about this before you make a decision that might invalidate that insurance policy.

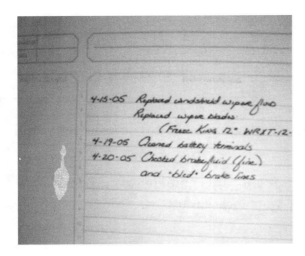

Fig. 1-3: Keeping your own notebook of parts, repairs, and maintenance helps you locate the right part and process later on.

KEEPING YOUR OWN RECORD

In discussing the owner's manual, I told you that the manual often includes a section where you can record your routine maintenance history, such as when you changed your oil and when you replaced your brakes. But the tiny space some manuals offer may not be adequate.

Since my partner and I have been doing much of my own maintenance, we've found it enormously helpful to buy a small notebook that easily fits in the glove compartment in which we can jot down details like:

- parts purchased, including what we had originally and what we replaced it with;
- all maintenance procedures, including seasonal upkeep;
- small repairs we did ourselves;
- major repairs done elsewhere, including what was done, who did it, and whether the work was covered by the warranty; and
- mysterious little problems that seemed to resolve themselves.

This little notebook (figure 1-3) allows us to go back and find information about parts and repairs we've long since forgotten. Here's an example: One of our vehicles uses a really strange oil filter, and whenever we have to replace it as part of regular maintenance, it's a bear to find the right one because the replacement listed in most guides for our vehicle does not fit properly. The first few times we went through this, we ended up going back and forth to the store until we got the right one rather than the listed one. By recording this detail, we eliminated a lot of lost time because we know exactly which oil filter we need.

Also, when we have to take the vehicle in for a serious repair, we pull that notebook out to write down information from the mechanic such as symptoms to watch for or what we might need to do next. This notebook-turned-into-a-logbook has been invaluable because we can only remember so much.

You also may want to check out your local or online software store for applications designed for both desktops and notebooks that allow you to keep your vehicle maintenance records. Do a Google search (www.google.com) and you can find sites like carcaresoftware.com, TATEMS 2005, and AutoWolf programs, to name just a few.

Finally, keep a folder or a small box in which you stash all your receipts from repairs and maintenance along with those jobs you do yourself. You will be surprised how often this historical record of purchases and services will be helpful.

2 PUTTING TOGETHER YOUR FIX-IT KIT

◆ Determining the basic tools you need

◆ Shopping for extras

◆ Assembling a small emergency kit

◆ Finding the right space to work

Probably one of the biggest differences between a pro and an amateur, besides the issue of experience, is having access to the tools needed to get the job done. If you happen to know a dedicated do-it-yourselfer, whether in the areas of car, home, or computer repair, you may have noticed this person has a collection of special tools to help bridge the distance between amateur and pro.

The good news for you is that you don't need to get terribly fancy or necessarily spend a bundle of money in putting together a decent auto fix-it kit. In some cases, you can borrow tools from others or rent something you may use only occasionally. Or you can check garage sales and flea markets for bargain-priced used tools and equipment.

DECIDING ON THE BASICS OF YOUR GARAGE OR WORK SPACE

Unless you're planning to go into auto repair as a sideline business—which you probably aren't—you don't need a garage full of tools or even one of those big steel chests filled with an assortment of every tool you may ever possibly need. Instead, you need some essential general purpose tools, none of which you'll have to break the bank to acquire. Start with the following:

- At least two screwdrivers, one regular and one Phillips head, like the one shown in figure 2-1
- A selection of wrenches
- A small hammer for use more as a general implement than for serious pounding
- A pry bar (this can be anything useful for helping you pry something loose like a hub cap—the advantage of a pry bar over say, the head of a screwdriver is that you aren't as likely to damage either the tool or the object you're prying)
- A general-purpose work light (one of those caged hanging work lights that you can temporarily mount inside your hood, like that shown in figure 2-2, is ideal)
- A small but powerful handheld flashlight for spot illumination
- A general-purpose bucket or pail
- One or more shallow but wide containers that can be used as short-term holders for the oil you drain (get an idea of where your oil release valve is located because this may determine how tall a container you can fit beneath the vehicle)

If you borrow these tools from your general around-the-house tool collection, consider keeping them separate in your automobile work area so you can find them quickly when you need them. Also, auto repair and maintenance is dirty work and unless you're very good about cleaning your tools before returning them to a household drawer, you're going to carry grease and dirt back into the house. In addition, small children love tools. If you have them in your house you don't want those dirty tools ending up in their hands—or mouths.

Fig. 2-1: A Phillips screwdriver is easy to distinguish because it has an X-shaped head; trying to use a regular screwdriver on a Phillips-type screw can damage both the screw and the screwdriver.

Fig. 2-2: An example of a shop light that has a caged face to protect the bulb and a hook that allows you to hang it inside the hood or other space.

Be sure your tools are in good condition and that you replace them promptly once they become damaged. For example, a badly marred screwdriver head can quickly ruin the screws it's used on because it will strip metal away.

Additional Items to Have on Hand

Beyond the basics already described, there are some additional items you really should keep on hand when you work as well as some before-you-start considerations about the space in which you perform your repairs and maintenance. Later in this chapter, you'll find a list of recommended items to carry in the car with you in case of emergency. But some of those same items should also be available to you at home or in your garage for those times when you're working on your vehicle.

These include the following:

- The owner's manual discussed in chapter 1 along with any other reference material about your particular make and model, as well as the details of the warranty, if any, for your vehicle
- A fire extinguisher rated to deal with fires caused by combustible fuels
- A basic first-aid kit (the cuts and scratches you get from working with grease, corrosion, and metal need to be cleaned and dressed promptly)
- A tire gauge to measure the usable tread left on your tires as well as the tire pressure
- A rubber mallet, which can come in handy when trying to get recalcitrant yet delicate parts back into place

- A small, stiff-bristled brush that can be used to clean rust and gunk from surfaces like battery terminals
- A can of WD-40 lubricant as well as basic machine oil to lubricate squealing auto door hinges and other parts
- The right type of fluids and lubricants needed to top off or replace those used in your vehicle, including oil, brake fluid, automatic transmission fluid, antifreeze, and water for your radiator, distilled water to replace low water levels in nonsealed auto batteries, and windshield wiper fluid; these should all be specified in your owner's manual
- A good degreaser/cleaner like Simple Green (this is particularly good because it does an effective job and is nowhere near as damaging to the environment as many other cleaning agents)

Other useful additions to your collection include the following:

- A battery charger (see figure 2-3)
- Safety or shop glasses
- A flexible flashlight like a "snake" light you can temporarily wrap or place in tight spaces to give you extra light
- A box fan—even an old but working one—you can use in your garage to direct exhaust and fumes out of the space
- A selection of clean, low-lint rags

Also, besides the other lights discussed, I like to have a small but extremely powerful general light like the one pictured in figure 2-4 that isn't connected by a power cord to an electrical out-

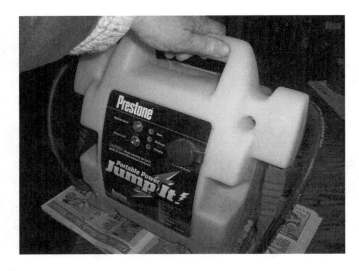

Fig. 2-3: A Prestone electrical charger that can be hooked up to a dead battery to restore the charge. Most chargers cost between $45 and $150.

Fig. 2-4: A powerful cordless spotlight can be helpful for daytime repairs as well as for emergency nighttime repairs. This one is small enough to fit in some glove compartments. It can also be stashed in the trunk or an emergency kit. Most models cost between $15 and $30 and can be recharged at any time.

let. This kind of light offers the power of a million candles in a very small package and has no cord to trip over.

Why the multiple lights? Because using just one or two light sources can create shadows. Until you're very accustomed to the inside or underside of your vehicle (and as a more casual repair person, you may never be that familiar with your car), you stand a much greater risk of breaking something, not seeing a problem like a loose or cracked hose, or injuring yourself if you don't have adequate illumination.

If you need a special tool, call your local auto parts store. Some will rent equipment and/or let you use the tool at their site. The fee may be by the hour or by the day. Some may require a deposit on a credit card (a debit card usually works, too) for security in case you trash the tool or fail to return it.

Adequate Space

Having adequate space to do your repairs and maintenance work is a big deal. If you have a garage at home, that can help quite a lot, especially when you're doing maintenance and fixes during bad weather.

But even when you have a garage, you should try to make certain you have enough space to work. All too often, our garages are so filled to overflowing with boxes, bikes, and equipment such as lawnmowers and snow blowers that they becomes too cramped to walk around in, let alone provide elbow room to work. So clear some space.

There are little wheeled platforms you can buy to enable you to roll under a vehicle and roll out

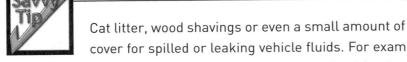

Cat litter, wood shavings or even a small amount of straw can be helpful as a short-term cover for spilled or leaking vehicle fluids. For example, when I had a car that leaked tiny amounts of oil when I parked it in the garage, the first thing I would do is throw some self-clumping cat litter on the spots. The litter would absorb most of the oil, making the rest of the mess much easier to clean up.

again. These are not particularly expensive, but unless you plan to work under your car frequently (and you probably don't), I'm not sure they're worth it. And until you get used to using one, they can actually make it easier to bang your head or arm as you try to wheel in and out.

Because you're working with tools, sharp parts and sometimes toxic fluids, it's a good idea to keep kids and pets out of your work area. More than one dog, unfortunately, has decided to taste spilled antifreeze fluid (which is poisonous to animals and humans) and more than one child has slipped on a tiny oil slick.

Also consider lighting. Not all garages are well lit and you want decent lighting when you're trying to spot or fix problems. Even though you've now learned the importance of additional lighting with flashlights and work lights, good overall lighting is important, too.

Finally, be sure you've got adequate ventilation. Without it, fumes from starting the vehicle can build up and not only give your lungs a workout but can also lead to an unnecessary headache or feeling of fuzziness. Wherever possible, don't just pop open a single window. Instead, try to open two windows at different parts of the work space or a door and a window so that there is cross ventilation, making it less likely that carbon monoxide and other fumes, will get trapped in an area where they can't dissipate. A box fan positioned in front of the vehicle that blows back toward the open window or garage door is also a good idea.

Keep your garage free of flammables. Sure, we've all seen a mechanic light up a cigarette while working on a vehicle. But it's ill-advised. One spark at the wrong time can be trouble.

What if you don't have a garage? Well, the work becomes a little tougher but is by no means impossible. Your best bet is a very level blacktop area. If you don't want to mess up your driveway blacktop with possible oil or other stains, you can buy a mat on which your vehicle can be placed while you work. A cardboard box cut to lie flat works well, too.

Grassy areas are a bad idea for a number of reasons. For one, they're less apt to be level. For another, you don't want spilled or leaking fluids to go into the ground and possibly into the ground water, resulting in contamination. It's not too unusual to see bald spots develop in the grass where you work. But you also want to avoid spills and leaks even if you're just working on dirt because the fluid can still leach into the ground.

Also, grassy areas can often be damp from dew in the morning, making it uncomfortable if you have to get down on your knees or sit on the ground; this also increases the chance that you could slip. Finally, it's easier to lose small parts or tiny tools, especially if the grass is not kept very short. While you can always get a large mat or tarp on which you can put your vehicle while you work, this won't help much if the ground isn't level.

If all else fails, you might ask a neighbor friend, or family member for temporary use of a free garage bay if you just don't have the right work space available to you at home.

Renting Garage Space

Some people, when first getting into doing their own vehicular repairs, find themselves wishing they could just rent a bay in a professional car shop for a day. Indeed, if you look around, you may be able to find a place that lets you do just that, charging you a flat rate either per hour or per day.

Understand, though, that unless you're an experienced mechanic (which you probably aren't), having that deep pit you can jump down into or a hydraulic lift so you can send your buggy up several feet into the air so you can work beneath the vehicle may not be quite the huge advantage you're hoping for. For one thing, most of the kind of repairs for which this kind of access would be helpful are generally out of the league of the non-pro. But a bigger cause for concern is the safety issue. Even grizzled veteran repair pros get hurt climbing in and out of the pits— which can also get pretty greasy, too, and more than one vehicle has slipped off a hydraulic lift.

If for some reason you feel compelled to try your own repairs using one of these rented bays, then do yourself a favor and read closely any paperwork you're asked to sign. As you can probably imagine, insurance companies are not too keen on the idea of nonprofessionals using equipment meant for those with more experience. So most places that will rent you this kind of garage space are going to want you to waive your right to sue if something happens, whether or not that something is an accident you cause.

YOUR IN-CAR EMERGENCY KIT

Beyond what you keep at home for repairs and maintenance, it's pretty important that you keep at least a basic emergency kit in your vehicle at all times to cope with problems that come up.

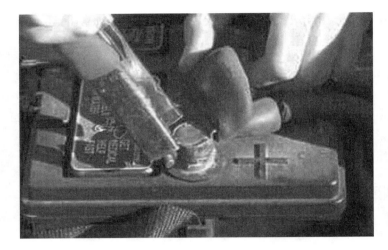

Fig. 2-5: Jumper cables are a must for any vehicle. Even if you don't feel comfortable using them, you want them on hand in case someone stops to assist you who doesn't have his or her own set.

Now, under most conditions, you don't want to be performing repairs alongside a busy roadway. If your car breaks down at night, this makes a tough situation nearly impossible. Instead, you may have to plan to sit tight until you can get a tow truck to retrieve you and your vehicle. So you'll see that the emergency kit includes some specialty items that can help you survive if you're stuck in the cold.

Your basic emergency kit should include the following:

- Jumper cables (see figure 2-5)
- Screwdriver and wrench
- Electrical or duct tape
- Can of temporary tire-patch spray
- Flashlight
- Emergency light and/or road flare(s)
- Bandages or small first aid kit
- One or more clean, sturdy rags
- An assortment of wire ties to help you secure things

Package these items up together rather than let them roll around loose under a seat or in the trunk. You also want to position these out of children's reach and keep them from being exposed to severe heat or cold. An old canvas tote or zippered bag can be ideal as a case for your kit.

As you put this emergency kit together, stop and think about past emergencies you've had, especially with your current vehicle. Consider what would have helped you in a prior situation and be sure you include it in your kit.

Obviously, a charged cell phone can be a lifesaver. For this reason, always invest in a phone charger that allows you to recharge the unit from the car.

If you've got the space—or can make the room by cleaning out the rear seat or trunk—there are some other items that make very savvy additions to your emergency vehicle kit. These items include the following:

- Spare jacket (both for warmth and to be pressed into service to cover your good clothes while you perform an on-the-spot repair)
- Blanket
- Fire extinguisher (get one rated for the kind of fires you can have with an auto)
- Small supply of food (energy bars or something else that can keep you going if you're stuck without assistance for several hours)
- Bottle of water (this can be used for everything from adding water to a radiator to helping you clean your hands to drinking)
- Disposable camera

Why a disposable camera? This is useful if you're involved in an accident. Being able to take photos of the situation before one or both vehicles get moved can help explain what happened to an insurance company or to police trying to understand who's at fault or which vehicle is responsible for a particular bit of damage.

Also plan to check your emergency kit on a regular basis—at least once every three or four months. You want to be sure the kit isn't missing something because someone borrowed an item from it. You'll also want to replace the small supply of food and water. Remember, too, that anything battery-powered will only last so long, even if the batteries aren't used. So test the flashlight.

Someone may have told you always to carry around a small amount of gasoline. This is not a great idea. Most gas containers are large, which means people often use smaller, nonstandard containers that may not be clearly labeled and could spill. Gas is flammable and dangerous. It should not be carried anywhere other than your fuel tank for anything other than very short periods of time.

Savvy Tip

You can find several models of these diagnostic code reader plugs that work with a handheld computer such as a Palm Pilot or a Windows CE system. Some permit you to plug your results directly into a desktop PC as well. Just be sure that the accompanying software works with your operating system (listed under System Requirements or Compatibility Checklist).

ABOUT PACKAGED KITS

You've learned in this chapter about how to put together an emergency kit. A slew of prepackaged kits are also available. Besides general tool kits, there are a multitude of specialty ones to address specific needs, like fixing cracks in a windshield, improving fuel consumption, and even performing winterization and other seasonal chores. There are also emergency kits that include first-aid items along with bottled water, a roll-up thermal blanket, and more.

Let's start with the prepackaged general kits. These often involve a small plastic or vinyl carry-all with a screwdriver, wrench, a can of temporary "fix-a-flat-tire" spray, maybe a tire gauge to help you tell when you need to add air to your tires, jumper cables, emergency flares, and other goodies. As you've learned, having something like this is pretty smart.

But be choosy about what you buy. Some of these kits include really cheap tools that break easily or that are too small to be a comfortable fit in your hand, making them difficult to use. Also, these kits may sit on a store shelf for months if not years before someone buys them, and that's not necessarily good. A can of spray to temporarily patch a deflating tire may not last forever. Likewise, the disposable lights some kits include may no longer work when you finally press them into service. So if you buy a kit—or put one together yourself—check their contents occasionally to be sure everything in there is still in good, usable condition. Also be sure no one has borrowed some tool from that kit and not replaced it.

When it comes to these kits, it becomes extremely important to:

- be wary of incredible claims;
- be certain you understand how to perform the repair; and
- be prepared to get your vehicle to a professional if the results aren't what you expected.

Take the case of a windshield or fuel tank repair kit. Both windshields and fuel tanks perform a very necessary purpose. You do not want to be going down the highway at 55 miles per hour and have a small crack or hole suddenly turn into a shattered windshield that, at best, you can't see out of or, at worst, may come flying back into your face. You wouldn't believe how much force is exerted against your windshield as you drive. Combine that force with winter's harsh cold and you can have a tiny crack turn into a broken pile of hundreds of little chips in no time. A couple of winters ago, a pebble from the road flew up and registered a dent in my windshield so small I could barely see it. The very next day, in subzero temperatures, I had driven no more than a few miles when that almost imperceptible ding transformed itself into a jagged crack that ran the full length of the windshield.

Likewise, gas is extremely flammable. You don't want to risk that a leak can get out of control or come into contact with a spark or a cigarette tossed out of another car's window.

In both cases, it's smarter to have a pro take care of these problems for you rather than buy a special use kit hoping to save yourself a repair bill. Doing the repair incorrectly—or ignoring the situation—can place you and your passengers in danger.

A Tool to Let Your Car Tell You What's Wrong

As our vehicles became smarter through computerization and a greater emphasis on electronics, auto troubleshooting and repair has gotten smarter, too. In recent years, you may have noticed that when you take your vehicle into the shop, the mechanics plug it into a console or use a handheld device that allows them to read information from your onboard computer. Some of the details they get are the diagnostic trouble codes (DTCs) I discussed briefly in chapter 1.

The great news for those of us without access to a fully equipped repair shop is that many companies now offer handheld, consumer versions of these diagnostic plug-in devices to check and display codes for problems with cars. You then look up the codes in your owner's manual or online through the manufacturer's Web site to determine what these codes mean. You'll learn more about using these devices as we get farther along in our work together.

The cost of these diagnostic plug-in tools can vary from $60 on up into the hundreds. The more advanced the gadget is, of course, the more expensive it will be. If you really can't afford one or don't want to fork over that much, you may be able to rent such tools from an auto parts store or rental center. Some garages will even run the diagnostic tests for a small fee, regardless of whether you plan to let them do any needed repairs. Likewise, I've dealt with some auto parts stores that will send a clerk out to your vehicle to check the codes and review the problems with you so you can determine what parts you may need to fix the trouble.

Thinking Ahead: Cleanup and Disposal

One thing you have to stop and think about before doing your own maintenance and repairs is how you'll deal with the leftovers and the mess. This isn't just about aesthetics, either.

As mentioned before, many of the fluids used in your car are not environmentally friendly. One fast way to waste the money you've just saved on your self-maintenance, for example, is to have to call a plumber because you thought it was acceptable to pour waste oil down the sink or flush greasy paper towels down the toilet. While you can store waste fluids for the short term in a container in your garage until you figure out what else to do with them, you run the risk of a fire or that a child or pet will get into them at some point. Or you could accidentally topple the container, creating a whole new mess.

Check with your local municipality. Many of them offer—usually in conjunction with a state or federal program—hazardous waste or special household waste collection events where you can dispose of everything from old car batteries and waste oil to bald tires and other replaced auto parts.

If they don't offer a program, then your next call should be to your garbage carrier, which may let you dispose of this material under special conditions—you may have to drive it to a particular location or package it separately from your normal household waste. Some commercial garages and auto parts stores will also take your waste, including fluids; some charge a fee while others do not. Remember, too, that you will need a suitable container in which to transport the material.

If all else fails, contact your state's environmental protection agency (usually named the Department of Environment Protection or DEP in the government listings in your local phone book).

There is often a fee attached for turning in old batteries, tires, and even leftover antifreeze and oil. Some programs charge $1 per tire or $5 per battery, but many offer specials where you can turn in several items for a maximum fee of $5 or $10.

3 PLAYING DETECTIVE UNDER THE HOOD

- ◆ Opening the hood
- ◆ Identifying major structures and connections
- ◆ Checking your oil and other vital fluids
- ◆ Topping off your fluid levels
- ◆ Looking at hoses and connections

Don't let anyone fool you: not everyone knows what to expect upon opening the hood of his or her vehicle. Whether you're male or female, there are plenty of people just like you who don't know most of what is under there.

Men have it tougher, however, because they're *expected* to know. That's why you see so many men open the hood as if by reflex when there's a problem, then peer around suspiciously for what could be wrong. If they don't do it, others wonder what's wrong with them.

Yet the problem is the same for everyone: how do you identify what is wrong if you don't understand what you're looking at? In fact, the time to acquaint yourself with your vehicle is before you have an emergency so you understand how things should look and can appreciate the changes that may result from some form of vehicular malfunction.

This chapter is designed to give you a sense of the structures found beneath the hood, what

Do yourself a huge favor and whenever you buy a new vehicle—whether brand-new or new to you—immediately pull out the owner's manual and try to identify components under the hood. At this point, the engine will be about as clean as it gets and probably things are in fairly good shape. As you learned elsewhere, it makes your life so much easier if you familiarize yourself with how things like hoses, connections, and the overall arrangement should look so you can better identify a problem later on. I've even gone so far as to take digital pictures of the more unusual-looking parts under my hood—things not connected, for example—so I have them later for comparison purposes when I'm troubleshooting.

should be checked, and how you can identify a problem and correct it. You'll see how to check your oil and add a quart as needed, top off your windshield wiper fluid, find your radiator, and much more. You will also be treated to some tips on making your vehicular exploration easier.

Understand, however, that vehicles can be wildly different, even among different years of the same model. So take what you learn here and apply it to specific information about your vehicle, such as you will find in the owner's manual and in special references like a Chilton's or Haynes manual.

ANATOMY OF YOUR VEHICLE BENEATH THE HOOD

Let's be honest upfront. There is no generic diagram that will tell you exactly what everything is beneath the hood of your own particular vehicle. The changes—your car, truck, van, or SUV has undergone since you first purchased it—the accumulation of dirt, debris, grease, and carbon as well as repairs—can make it almost impossible to tell what everything is beneath the hood. Even modifications to a single model that a manufacturer often makes from year to year can switch all the components around.

If you find yourself unable to identify everything beneath your hood once you go through your references and this book, make it a point the next time you visit your local garage to have the mechanic take you on a tour of your under-the-hood structures. You can also call upon a knowledgeable friend, family member, neighbor, or work associate to do this.

Identifying and Locating Fluids You Need to Check

Most vehicles contain several fluids that perform various functions. These fluids include the following:

- Oil to lubricate the moving parts of your engine
- Brake fluid to lubricate your brakes
- Transmission fluid (on automatic transmissions only)
- Water in the cells of some types of vehicle batteries
- A mixture of water and coolant in your radiator.
- A water-and-solvent mix that you can spray on the windshield while driving

It is imperative that you follow your owner's manual recommendations as to how often you should check and drain/replace these fluids as well as the exact type of fluid replacement to use. Failure to do so can prove to be very expensive, since you can have a breakdown of the hardware involved.

WARNING: Also check your owner's manual to determine if your vehicle has one or more additional types of fluid levels you need to monitor and refill as needed. Some air-conditioning systems, for example, may require a special fluid that is added at the beginning of warm weather.

About Checking Your Oil

Automotive professionals are constantly amazed not only at how few drivers realize how simple it is to check the oil level in their vehicles but also at how few understand that this procedure is critical. The simple failure to check oil ruins engines across the country every day. In my college days, I had three different friends ruin otherwise great cars just because they never checked their oil—and one of those vehicles was just a few months old.

Your owner's manual should specify exactly what viscosity—thickness—of oil your vehicle needs. Use what is recommended. If you have two or three vehicles, make sure you use the right type for each vehicle rather than buying the same for all and hoping for the best. Don't decide to switch viscosities just because you see a great sale on oil. In fact, some pros recommend that you stick with the same oil brand and type throughout the life of your vehicle.

Many mechanics suggest you check the oil with every gas fill-up. Most people, however, can get by with doing this every week or two, though you should bump up your oil checks whenever:

- you're about to take a long trip in the vehicle;

If you've got a vehicle that burns a fair amount of oil but you're not ready to send it to the garage for an engine analysis and overhaul, consider always carrying an extra quart of oil in the trunk.

- you begin to drive a great deal more on a regular basis;
- you notice the level is getting low but not quite to the point where you need to add oil yet; or
- you notice that the vehicle is burning more oil than usual, which happens with many older vehicles or those in dire need of engine work.

Also, besides performing regular checks, you should consult your owner's manual to learn how frequently you should change the oil in your vehicle. Again, this is usually based on mileage or a specific number of months, whichever occurs first. Chapter 5 explains how to do this job yourself.

Normally, you should check your oil when the engine is warm because the results are likely to be more accurate. Follow these steps:

1. Open your hood.
2. Locate your oil indicator or dipstick, usually positioned near the oil fill cap.
3. Remove the dipstick and wipe it down with a cloth or paper towel.
4. Reinsert the dipstick as straight and evenly as possible to its full length, then pull it out again, also trying to keep the stick straight.

Fig. 3-1: Position the dipstick so you can clearly see its markings. Consult your owner's manual as needed.

WHY ADDING TOO MUCH OIL ISN'T MUCH BETTER THAN RUNNING WITH TOO LITTLE

At the opposite end of the spectrum from those drivers who almost never check their oil levels are those who decide that if too little oil is bad, too much is a great idea. It's not.

Your engine is designed to run with the correct amount of oil. If it has to operate with too little, then the engine can seize, the rods inside can deform, and the engine can literally burn itself up. Yet too much oil transforms your exhaust into greasy clouds that could result in an engine fire. Flooding your engine with oil your car can't use can result in damage about as extensive as the "too little" scenario.

Instead, strike a happy medium. Check your oil regularly and add a quart when your dipstick indicates the level is low. Keep a quart on hand, but only add it when needed.

---

5. Check to see the level at which the oil appears, as shown in figure 3-1. Different dipsticks may use slightly different indicators, but most have marks showing a "full" level when no oil is needed and an "add" level when a quart is needed. If the level appears fine, jump to step seven. If not, move to the next step.

6. If the level appears particularly low, you may need to add more than one quart. To add oil, reinsert the dipstick and then remove the oil cap as shown in figure 3-2. Taking care not to spill the fluid, add one quart, then recheck the level using the dipstick. If it still appears low, add a half quart more and check again, repeating these steps until there is the correct amount of oil. Replace the oil cap when you're finished adding oil.

7. Reinsert the dipstick.

Fig. 3-2: Locate and remove your oil fill cap. This is where you will add any oil needed to reach an acceptable level as shown on your oil dipstick.

Don't assume that oil is supposed to appear black. In fact, good grade oil should look amber-colored and be fairly translucent when you check your oil dipstick. If your oil seems especially thick (or thin), not translucent, or black, it's time for an oil change. If you have recently changed your oil but it still looks opaque, you probably want a mechanic to perform a thorough check of your engine. It's possible some fouled part of the system is corrupting the oil much more quickly than is normal

WARNING: What if no oil appears on your dipstick when you check it? The best thing to do is recheck the oil level. It's also possible you need to take the reading of the dipstick in better light; clean oil may be more difficult to see. If no oil is present even on a recheck, then you need to add oil immediately. Once you have added a few quarts, check the dipstick again and keep adding a quarter (or half) quart at a time until the dipstick reads in the proper range. If it never does, call a mechanic immediately. If, instead, your oil dipstick indicates there is too much oil present, and rechecking confirms this, you may need to drain at least a small volume of oil. Consult the instructions in chapter 5 for performing an oil change to learn how to drain oil.

Looking at Brake Fluid

Because your brakes include moving parts—several of them—they require lubrication, which is the job of brake fluid. Your job is to routinely check the brake fluid to see whether the level needs replenishment.

If it does require filling, use the exact type of brake fluid specified in your owner's manual, since that's what the manufacturer believes works best for your type of hydraulic brake system. This is critical, because different brake types demand various types of fluid, ranging from glycol-based to silicon-based formulations; some absorb water and some don't. Using the wrong kind could spell bad news for brake operation and life. The fluid, too, plays a role in how well the brake pedal compresses when you step on it.

How frequently you should do this check also depends on the vehicle type. Some manufacturers recommend checking it monthly, while many manufacturers feel that once every 3,000 miles—or at the time of your regular oil change—is sufficient.

WARNING: Be very careful when handling brake fluid. Some types will actually destroy the finish on your automobile and some people may have a strong reaction if they get it on

their skin. This fluid isn't very environmentally friendly, either, as you might expect from something that can eat paint.

Brake fluid is stored in—and added to—the master cylinder reservoir. Again, your owner's manual should specify where this is located and what you need to do. Some later-model vehicles have a smaller reservoir attached to the master cylinder that enables you to see the fluid level at a glance. You can unsnap the reservoir cap to add fluid as needed.

This is the basic process for checking your brake fluid:

1. Locate the brake fluid check area.
2. Clean this area with a cloth so you don't introduce dirt and grease into the reservoir when you open it.
3. Remove the lid—sometimes done by unsnapping a bail that is in place—and lift it off as shown in figure 3-3.
4. Check the markers on the reservoir, using a flashlight if necessary, to determine the current fluid level and the recommended level.
5. If the current level is below the recommended level, add the specified brake fluid until you see that the proper level is reached.
6. Replace the brake reservoir cover.

You may notice a diaphragm inside the reservoir. This acts as a barrier so loose dirt and debris cannot make their way into the reservoir itself. On some vehicles, you may have to lift or remove the diaphragm to check the fluid level—consult your manual for details.

Fig. 3-3: Open the brake fluid reservoir cover. When you add the fluid, use extreme care not to spill it. Also, do not overfill.

Got Automatic Transmission Fluid (ATF)?

Not every vehicle has transmission fluid you can service yourself. For example, most manual transmission vehicles do not, while those with automatic transmissions usually do. Check your owner's manual to be sure, as well as to learn exactly what type of transmission fluid is recommended.

Transmission fluid should be checked once a month. The process for doing this is much like the oil check you performed earlier. Like with motor oil, you should not operate the vehicle with the transmission fluid low and you should not overfill it, either.

The check should be done with the engine warm. You should engage your parking brake and open your hood. Have a cloth or paper towel handy.

Then follow these steps:

1. Locate the transmission fill cap and the transmission dipstick under the hood.
2. Remove the transmission dipstick from its well and wipe it dry.
3. Replace the dipstick in its well and then pull it out very straight.
4. Look at the dipstick to see what level of fluid it registers. If it appears full, replace the dipstick and close the hood. You're done. If not, proceed to step 5.
5. Remove the transmission fill cap and set it aside.
6. Carefully pour a bottle of transmission fluid (using the type specified in your owner's manual) into the fill container.
7. Recheck the fluid level. Once it shows as full, you can replace the fill cap and dipstick and close the hood.

How's Your Power Steering Fluid Level?

If your vehicle has power steering—which means you don't have to work so hard at turning the wheel, since the car provides assistance—you may need to check your power steering fluid level and add fluid, if indicated. If you don't have power steering, you don't need to worry about this.

Checking Water/Coolant Levels in the Radiator

The radiator usually sits at the very front of the car (as seen in figure 3-4), just behind the grille, which serves as the "face" of the vehicle between the headlights. At the top of the radiator is a pressure release cap (figure 3-5). Somewhere close to the radiator on many makes and models is a mostly transparent reservoir, sometimes called the coolant overflow or "slosh" tank, where excess fluid resides when it's not demanded by the cooling system.

Fig. 3-4: The radiator in a Suzuki Sidekick. At the top is the pressure release valve, which should be opened with extreme care when the vehicle is hot. Fluid can spray up from an overheating radiator and the pressure can be so great as you release the cap that the cap can be blown from your grip.

Fig. 3-5: The coolant overflow or "slosh" tank is usually found near the radiator. Unlike the pressure cap on the radiator itself, you can usually pop open the overflow tank lid safely and easily.

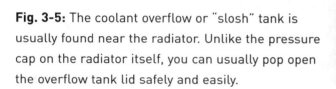

If you ask most people what goes into a radiator for fluid, they are likely to say "antifreeze" or "water." But in truth, it's usually a careful 50-50 mix of antifreeze or coolant and water. A thermostat under the hood watches the operating temperature of the vehicle and calls for adjustment of coolant mixture to supply more or less, as needed, to meet the demands of the current situation.

Over time, the coolant can degrade, no longer providing the same degree of protection from extreme operating temperatures that it does when it is first added. Dirt in the system and buildup in the radiator also act to contaminate the fluid mix. You begin to exhaust the water-coolant mix so the level in the system begins to go down, too.

Check your water/coolant levels at least once a month. It's not a bad idea to check more often when:

- your area is experiencing very high temperatures; and

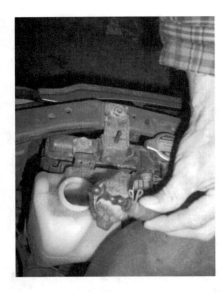

Fig. 3-6: The coolant tank makes it much easier to add water and coolant than pouring the liquids into the radiator itself. You also don't risk damaging the radiator.

- you notice the vehicle's dashboard temperature gauge is reading higher than usual, especially when you're sitting idling in traffic or parked.

Beyond this, you should flush your radiator at least twice a year or as frequently as recommended in your owner's manual. (Chapter 5 tells you how to do this.) This operation both refreshes the coolant/water mixture and removes any dirt or debris that has gotten into the cooling system.

Speaking of coolant, most of us are accustomed to radiator fluid or antifreeze that is colored an almost fluorescent yellow-green. But this is just one of the many types available now. The color of newer antifreeze formulas may range from shades of rose or orange to deep, dark red. You can also notice color variations once the antifreeze is mixed with water and after it has been in use for some period of time. These formulas reflect some of the changes that have been made in automotive heating and cooling systems. They are often far more tolerant of temperature extremes than their predecessors.

Here's how to check the fluid level:

1. Open the hood.
2. Locate the coolant overflow tank.
3. Look at the markings on the overflow tank to determine whether the current level is adequate. If it is, you're finished until your next check. If the level is low, go to step 4.
4. Unsnap the cap on the coolant tank as shown in figure 3-6.
5. Add a mix of coolant and water as specified in your owner's manual.

WHAT TO DO WHEN YOUR VEHICLE OVERHEATS

If you haven't experienced an overheating vehicle yourself, you've no doubt seen one on TV or in a movie, where billowing white smoke enshrouds the car and the driver gets frustrated as he carelessly pulls off the radiator cap.

Usually, long before a vehicle reaches the "steaming mimi" stage, you'll notice that the temperature gauge on the dashboard is creeping ever higher. Sometimes, the only surprise is how quickly many vehicles can go from a normal temperature to a situation where a radiator is boiling over like a giant tea kettle.

When your vehicle is operating in the fever range, pull over and stop the car for several minutes. Pop the hood but don't touch anything yet. Just let it—and you—cool down a few degrees.

Then check the fluid level in your coolant overflow tank. If that tank shows empty—always a possibility in this situation—you need to fill the tank to the proper level with water only. If you're on the road a distance from home, make your next stop a place where you can buy a jug of water or two to keep in the vehicle in case you need to add water again; you should recheck the tank level regularly and add more water as required until the temperature returns to normal.

Do not keep driving for any period of time if the temperature remains high; you want a garage to check the cooling system and determine what's wrong. This could be a busted radiator hose, a hole or crack in the radiator itself, or a stuck or broken thermostat, to name a few possibilities.

Once the emergency has passed and the car is cool, you can refill the tank with a proper mix of coolant and water.

---

6. Wipe away any spilled mixture.
7. Replace the tank cap and close the hood.

Does Your Battery Need Water?

Standard car batteries tend to fall into two basic categories:

- those that require a certain amount of maintenance; and
- those that demand no maintenance whatsoever.

Your first job is to determine which type you have. Your owner's manual or the literature that accompanied a replacement battery should tell you exactly what is required in the way of maintenance, if anything.

Examining the battery can also give you a hint. If the battery appears completely sealed and there is no access panel so you can reach the cells, you probably have a no-maintenance battery.

However, your battery could be just dirty enough to make it difficult to tell exactly what you have. Just as you might guess, a dirty battery should be cleaned because debris can interfere with the current that must run from the battery into your electrical and ignition system to supply juice as you start the vehicle.

Chapter 5, where you learn more of the important components of routine maintenance, details both how to clean up your battery as well as how you can add water to the cells on a regular (rather than a maintenance-free) vehicle battery.

How About Your Windshield Wiper Fluid Level?

Finally, you've reached the easiest fluid to check and change: the fluid used by your car to pump a mix of water and solvent up onto the windshield to clear the glass. This is the one fluid most people know they must add, and they usually do.

But just in case you haven't done this before, let's go over the steps. Again, you should consult your owner's manual both to determine the location of your windshield fluid reservoir and what type of fluid mix you should use.

Do this:

1. Open your hood and locate your windshield fluid reservoir.
2. Use the markings on the outside of the tank to determine whether the level is adequate. If it is, you don't need to do anything else but close the hood. If you need to add fluid, proceed to step 3.
3. Unsnap the cap usually found at the top of the reservoir.
4. Add washer fluid until the tank shows the correct level.
5. Replace the cap and close the hood.

In chapter 5, you'll learn how to flush your radiator and replace its mix of coolant and water.

When operating a vehicle in very cold weather, you want a windshield fluid that contains alcohol or another substance to reduce the chance the fluid will freeze and become unusable.

CHECKING HOSES, BELTS, AND CONNECTIONS

Anytime you are under your hood, it's a great opportunity to examine your hoses, belts, and connections to make certain they are securely in place and free of any damage or severe wear and that there are no obvious signs of a leak or slackness. For best results, you should do this while the vehicle is cool so you won't get burned.

As I mentioned earlier, if you make a point of checking your system when everything works, you'll have a much better idea of how things should look. If you took the suggestion to take a photograph or two of the engine while it was clean and (at least relatively) new, you can refer to this to try to evaluate any changes or loose connections that might be present.

If you notice a small rip or tear in a hose, you may be able to patch it up temporarily with heat-tolerant tape. However, you should drive to the auto parts store as soon as possible and see if there's a replacement hose you can install yourself. If not, you may want to take the vehicle to a mechanic.

Check connections like those that run from the cylinders and spark plugs to the distributor cap, the battery, and other parts of the engine compartment. If you see something questionable, consult your owner's manual to try to determine what the part or hose is and how it should look.

Try to make a point of checking all your belts at least monthly to avoid a situation where one breaks or otherwise gives way when you're out on the road. Any belts that are damaged (badly worn, frayed, or separating) should be replaced immediately. Loose belts with a half inch or more of slack can usually be tightened with a screwdriver or other tool. You can touch the belt—like this fan belt shown in figure 3-7—to see if you can detect any slack.

Fig. 3-7: Inspect the fan belt and other belts for signs of wear, tear, or looseness.

4 SCOPING OUT THE EXTERIOR

◆ Checking for external signs of trouble

◆ Performing your own vehicle inspection

◆ Gauging your tires

◆ Testing your lights and horn

◆ Coping with early signs of rust

◆ Peeking under the vehicle

◆ Getting a whiff of your exhaust

◆ Looking for leaks and drips

◆ Lubricating noisy door hinges

The more time you spend around your vehicle, the less likely you are to see it with critical eyes. This means simply that you're so used to seeing it that it becomes harder for you actually to notice something that is not quite right.

Yet even the exterior of your vehicle can give you some clues about its overall condition. Going over your vehicle with an eye toward possible problems can help you identify issues you can anticipate and correct before they blow up into a major repair.

With this in mind, this chapter is devoted to helping you cast a critical eye as you perform a savvy person's inspection of your vehicle and fix problems you see. Here, you will learn how to test your various vehicle lights, check your exhaust, look for any signs of leaks, spot the first signs of rust, and much, much more.

While you go through this inspection, understand that it's smart to do something like this every four to six weeks. Doing this exterior survey, along with overall basic maintenance, is especially important before you take an extended trip in your vehicle or face some other situation where you depend on your vehicle even more heavily than usual.

BEFORE YOU START

Begin by parking your vehicle on as level a surface as possible, preferably outside your garage. Since you'll be running the engine for at least a short while during the inspection, you don't want exhaust fumes to build up inside a garage. If you must work with the vehicle inside, make certain you've got very good circulation, with windows and/or doors open and an exhaust fan on and pointed outdoors.

There are at least a couple of reasons for the level surface. You will be checking your tires as well as taking a look at how the vehicle sits. Both steps can be helped by having the vehicle sit as evenly as it normally would.

A clipboard with paper and pen or a notebook will be useful during this process (see figure 4-1). This way, you can take notes if you spot more issues than you are likely to remember. A flashlight to peer beneath the car isn't a bad idea either.

Also, for at least part of this exercise, it may be helpful if you can enlist the services of a friend, family member, or neighbor to watch for your brake lights and other lights as you test them. He or she can also be pressed into service to tell you how funky the first stream of exhaust appears when you start the vehicle, which can be a tell-tale sign of the need for an oil change or a deeper problem like a fouled engine or a damaged engine head.

How you perform your inspection is largely up to you. Here I suggest a systematic check that starts from a slight distance and then lets you move up close to look at different parts separately. The systematic method makes it less likely you'll miss something you need to see.

STEP 1: CHECK YOUR VEHICLE'S BALANCE

Stand about five to 10 feet of the front of your vehicle. If you parked the vehicle on a level surface, your vehicle should be seated fairly normally. If it's not, see if you can determine a reason why, like one tire being positioned on a rock or in a small depression.

Fig. 4-1: Unless you're lucky enough to find very little wrong, you may want to take notes as you look around. Doing so can prevent you from forgetting some details later on.

Yes, there's a reason for checking this: you want to tell if part of your vehicle is either elevated or sits below the rest of the vehicle, which may indicate bad shocks or a suspension problem that needs to be addressed, most likely by a professional mechanic.

Here's a simple test you can perform to check your vehicle's shock absorbers. Press down with both hands on both the hood and trunk of the vehicle, using some force. As soon as you stop "bouncing" the vehicle, it should quickly stop moving. If the car continues to bounce after you stop, this is a sign your shock absorbers are worn and may need replacement. Have a mechanic you trust check this for you.

STEP 2: LOOK OVER THE VEHICLE FRONT AND WINDSHIELD

Now step up close to the front of your vehicle. Look at the grille around the front. Is it covered with bugs and debris? If so, you probably want to clean it—not just for aesthetics, but because debris here prevents the heat from the engine from dissipating and also keeps cool air from flowing in where it can be picked up by your car's vents. Chapter 5 explains how to clean the grille and the front of the radiator.

Look at the windshield next. If there are any dings or cracks, note them. Even tiny pockmarks in the glass can turn into a shattered windshield if you don't get them repaired or the glass replaced before you rocket down a highway or drive the vehicle during extremes of tempera-

Savvy Tip

Car insurance often picks up most of the cost of window replacements, usually without driving up your insurance rates. Often, you end up paying between $50 and $100 out of your own pocket, at most. But if you've had a lot of claims recently with your car insurance company it might be wise to pay out of pocket for this repair. Call your insurance agent to find out if your rate will go up with a windshield claim.

ture. Also check the rubber-like seal around the windshield. Be sure it's not cracked or separating. If so, this needs to be glued down using special glue you can find at your auto parts store. If the seal goes too long without repair, it will need replacement, usually by a professional garage.

Do a similar check of other windows in your auto along with their seals. While the most stress is placed on the windshield as you drive, you don't want a situation where you lose any of your windows. Making certain the seals are in place and in good condition is one way to prevent this from happening.

While still working with your windows, check the well at the front of the car where your windshield wipers sit. Pull your wipers up to a vertical position and then clean this well out using a brush to remove debris as shown in figure 4-2.

Now look at the wiper blades themselves. Are the blades still in one piece? If not, or if you have noticed that they are no longer doing a good job of removing moisture from the windshield, they should be replaced. Your owner's manual should tell you the replacement blade type you need.

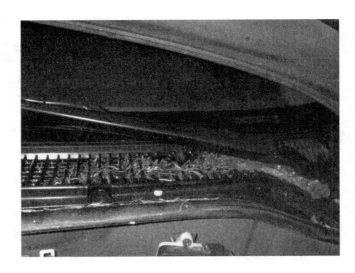

Fig. 4-2: You should regularly clean any dirt and debris that gets into the well where your wipers sit. If you don't, this debris gets caught in your wiper blades and can scratch the glass, ruin the wiper blades, and get sucked down into the air ducts of your vehicle.

Before you do this, you may want to thoroughly clean your windshield. This prevents the new blades from immediately picking up grit and other material that can ding the blade material.

Replacing wiper blades usually involves these steps:

1. Remove the clips that hold the current blade in place.
2. Slide off the existing blade.
3. Slip the new blade on.
4. Fasten it in place.

Step 3: Check the Vehicle Rear

Bend down and inspect the rear of the vehicle below the back bumper. Is anything hanging loose or hanging down, like the tailpipe? If so, using the owner's manual or any additional references you may have gotten for your particular make and model of vehicle, try to determine what it might be.

One of the most common things to hang loose is the exhaust pipe leading from the muffler. Yet you would be amazed at how many vehicle owners are saved the expense of replacing a muffler by buying something as simple as an inexpensive auto clamp (see figure 4-3) and reattaching a loose exhaust pipe before the assembly comes completely loose and falls off. You want to use a tape measure to gauge the width of the pipe and then go to your auto parts store to pick up the proper size clamp.

Step 4: Inspect Your Tires

Another reason you want to park your vehicle for the inspection on a fairly level surface is so you can look over your tires. Do they pouch out or otherwise appear soft? If so, they need to have air added to them. Your owner's manual will specify the exact pressure for your type of tire, which you shouldn't exceed when you go to a gas station and avail yourself of its air com-

It's smart to check your spare tire at the same time you perform your inspection. You'll also learn more about this in chapter 5, where you'll find the common steps involved in routine auto maintenance.

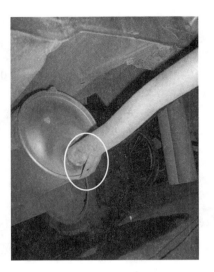

Fig. 4-3: If your muffler otherwise appears to be in good shape (no holes, no rust, no obviously broken parts), you may be able to clamp it back in place using an automotive clamp that costs under $3.

pressor. In the short term, you can hook up a home air compressor (see figure 4-4) or bicycle pump to add enough air to get safely to the gas station.

Now give your tires a closer look. How's the tread? You can purchase a tire gauge at the auto parts store that can help determine when it's time to replace the tires. If the tread, however, is almost gone, it's definitely time to replace your tires.

Is the tread unevenly worn? If so, it may be time for a wheel alignment. Chapter 5 talks more about this procedure, along with tire rotation—both jobs for a professional garage.

STEP 5: CHECK FOR RUST

Rust is a killer, eating away at the metal and weakening the physical integrity of the vehicle to the point where it can become a full-fledged safety hazard. It can occur even on vehicles that have been coated with rust proofing. Granted, changes in the materials used to manufacture cars, trucks, and SUVs—including both galvanized metals and, increasingly, plastics—are making rust less of an issue than ever before, but you still need to check for it.

> It's usually wise to replace all your tires at once rather than piecemeal unless early tire failures simply force you to have to buy tires individually. Tire rotation can prolong the life of your tires and prevent one or two tires from getting more wear than the others.

Fig. 4-4: A simple air compressor unit or a bicycle pump can be pressed into service to inflate a soft tire until you can get to a garage or gas station and have the tire filled to the correct pressure. Refer to your owner's manual for pressure requirements.

Some of the worst rust may happen where you cannot easily see it: on the underside of your vehicle, which is constantly exposed to moisture. In fact, you may not even realize you have a rust problem until you notice a sudden breeze enter the passenger compartment or the floorboard beneath your feet seems strangely weak.

Small dings and scratches anywhere on the vehicle body can also lead to rust. The very best thing you can do is perform a regular check of your vehicle for signs of rust. If you find any such rust spots, you should treat each one immediately before more damage can be done. However, if the rust is extensive, you need to consult a professional ASAP.

To treat smaller rust spots yourself, you will need a few tools:

- disposable gloves;
- an abrasive pad (those you use in the kitchen will work);
- sandpaper;
- can of rust converter/neutralizer;
- vehicle-quality sandable primer and/or rusty metal primer (available at your auto parts store);
- one or more small paint brushes of the right size for the spots;
- one or more clean, soft cloths;
- mineral spirits;
- newspaper (to spread beneath the vehicle where you're working);
- face mask or respirator (the fumes can be harsh especially if you need to apply paint); and
- protective glasses to prevent grit from getting in your eyes.

You may need some additional materials if the rust appears on the visible part of your vehicle, where there is paint involved. For example, let's say you have a scratch or chip with rust on the hood or bumper of your vehicle. If this is the case, you probably want to go the distance to both get rid of the rust and touch up the part so it looks much as it did before. For this, you need:

- auto body glazing putty
- clear coat spray
- touch-up paint (in the color of your vehicle—and many auto parts stores and dealers sell specific touch-up colors based on the exact shade of different makes/models of vehicles); and
- auto wax.

Let's tackle the small rust spots where you won't need to fix the paint job first:

1. If needed, spread newspaper below the area where you will work.
2. Remove any loose material around the rust spot.
3. Use the abrasive pad to carefully remove the visible rust.
4. Apply the rust converter/neutralizer with a brush and follow the package's instructions for how long to wait before proceeding with the next step. Usually, you want to wait two to three hours before you apply a second coat.
5. About 24 hours later, apply the primer according to package directions.
6. Depending on the instructions on the primer, wait however long is necessary before you clean up the area with a damp cloth and then wipe dry.

Now let's turn to a more serious spot or one where you need to fix up the appearance of the vehicle once you have removed the rust itself.

Follow these steps:

1. Use sandpaper or an abrasive pad to remove the rust.
2. Clean the area with a soft, dampened cloth once the rust is removed and then wipe dry.
3. Take the newspaper and, using scissors, cut out an area large enough to reveal the former rust spot (see figure 4-5). Then tape the newspaper in place, using masking tape, so that the hole is positioned over your work area.
4. Apply the primer according to package directions. You may need two to three coats, waiting at the intervals specified on the package. (See figure 4-6.)
5. Once the primer is dry and firm, use fine-grade sandpaper or an abrasive pad to smooth out the primer.
6. Use a plastic spreader to apply the automotive putty .
7. Once the putty is dry, wipe the area down with a dampened cloth and then dry.

Fig. 4-5: Cut out a large hole in a newspaper and position the hole over your work area. Then use masking tape to attach the newspaper to the vehicle. This helps keep the focus on the work area.

Fig. 4-6: For some reason, say many technicians and sales people, people seem to confuse primer with putty. Here, primer is being applied. Automotive putty is much finer than the type of putty you may have worked with for home repairs. Be sure you get the proper kind; you want the repair to look right.

8. Apply two to three coats of your touch-up paint, waiting for an interval between each coat as recommended on the paint container.
9. When the touch-up paint coats are dry, apply the clear top coat.
10. Once the top coat is dry, polish the area and then wax either just the area or your entire vehicle (after you've washed the vehicle, of course).

STEP 6: TEST YOUR LIGHTS AND HORN

A defective vehicle light isn't always just an inconvenience. A dead light can also be a safety hazard and could get you stopped by the police, especially if it's a critical light such as a headlight or a turn signal.

This part of the inspection is much easier if you have someone who can "spot" you as you test the lights. Start with the headlights and go through all of them, from the turn signals to the brake lights and parking lights. Don't forget the license plate light (police like to stop you when that one is out) or your interior lights, like the dashboard and dome. Test your hazard lights as well.

If any of the lights fail to work, look in your owner's manual to determine the replacement bulb or light type you need. Most manuals show you exactly how to replace important lights like the headlights. Most auto parts stores can easily look up the type you need and usually have the exact replacement type you need.

Sometimes it's a small fuse rather than a light that needs replacement. Many vehicles have a small fuse box (see figure 4-7) located under or near the bottom of the steering column or located under the hood where you can pull out tiny cylinder-style fuses and replace them (again, your auto parts store can help there).

While we've all known people who use their car horn way too much, many of us hardly if ever honk. But the horn is there for a reason: it can help you get attention when needed. For this reason, you should check the horn periodically to make certain it works.

STEP 7: HOW'S YOUR EXHAUST?

The exhaust that comes out when you first start your vehicle can actually be a powerful diagnostic tool about the condition of your vehicle. You should perform this test in the warm part of the day. On a cold morning you will often see plumes of exhaust, but this is usually just the result of condensation and the temperature differential and nothing to worry about.

Fig. 4-7: An underdash fuse box on a Suzuki Sidekick lets you check and replace individual fuses that control dash and console lights.

This is another part of the inspection where a helper comes in very handy. Have the person stand at the rear of the vehicle, just to the side, and watch the exhaust pipe as you start the engine.

If dark or bluish smoke comes out, this may be a sign of an engine burning a fair amount of oil, and possibly in need of a ring job, where the actual rings in the engine are adjusted. Clouds of dense white smoke, however, may indicate something wrong with the engine head, another big job that should be handled by a professional mechanic.

With the vehicle running, let it idle for a few minutes. How does it seem? If the vehicle keeps threatening to stall or otherwise seems to run very rough, it's probably time for a tune-up, especially if you haven't done one on this vehicle before or it has been a very long time since your last one. Chapter 6 shows you the basics of a tune-up, including changing your air filter and spark plugs.

Turn off the vehicle. Is there a residual chugging noise, almost like the engine is trying to turn over again? If so, the vehicle may need to have its timing adjusted or timing belt replaced. This again is usually a job for a professional mechanic because it involves special equipment—like a timing light—and a bit of experience.

GOT LEAKS?

If your vehicle isn't quite new anymore, there is always the possibility that you have a leak. This is especially true if you've noticed unexplained spots on the driveway or in the garage where you usually park.

Have an old sheet, huge bath towel, or something similar you can press into service? The lighter and plainer the color, the better. A roll of old shelving or wallpaper would also work for this.

Spread the sheet of paper, or even cardboard, under the vehicle (see figure 4-8), trying to cover the width from front to rear, left tire to right. Then start the vehicle and let it idle for about five minutes—not much longer than that.

Once you turn off the vehicle, pull the sheet or paper out and see if you notice any spots. A single drip here or there may not matter. But if there are several drops or a puddle, you may have a leak somewhere.

If you have a reference book for your make and model, try to determine which part of the vehicle corresponds to the area of the leak. Then schedule a garage visit for your vehicle as soon as possible—immediately if you have reason to believe the leak is gas or oil.

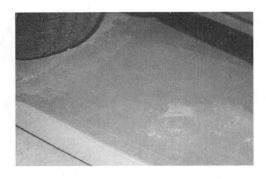

Fig. 4-8: Check for leaks by placing some sort of paper or old sheet or cardboard beneath the vehicle while it sits idling. Then inspect the paper or cloth for evidence of leaks.

Step 8: Oiling Squeaky Doors

Do you have one or more vehicle doors that sound like a special effects presentation for Halloween? Many of us do, even with vehicles that are not that old.

Unfortunately, many of us just grin and bear it, when a few drops of machine oil—like 3-in-One brand oil—applied to the hinge may not only reduce the dreadful sound but keep the door hinge working properly. If you don't lubricate the hinge, you could reach the point where it becomes very difficult to open or close the door.

Step 9: Wrap Up with the Little Things

Before you consider the inspection complete, go over the exterior of the vehicle once more looking for anything you might have missed. If you've been jotting down notes about problems encountered, mark off the ones you've repaired and circle the ones you need to address later or have checked by a mechanic.

As you go, look at the following:

- The vehicle mirrors—be sure they are firmly attached
- Your license plates—make certain one or both are present (depending on your state's laws), that they are firmly attached, and that they are clean
- Any inspection stickers required by your state or municipality—make sure they are up to date or make an appointment to get them up to date
- Your glove compartment—be sure you have your registration and insurance card
- Your in-vehicle emergency and repair kit—check to see that everything you need is there
- Your jack and spare tire—you don't want them missing at a crucial time

5 PRACTICING GOOD MAINTENANCE PREVENTS NASTY REPAIRS

◆ Building on what you know

◆ Identifying regular maintenance needs

◆ Things you need to check more or less frequently

◆ Looking for additional problems

◆ Seasonal maintenance

According to the Car Care Council, four out of every five vehicles don't receive regular maintenance. Without that tender loving care, those vehicles are likely to die an early death, but probably not before their owners shell out some big money for repairs they might have prevented if only they had taken the time for routine maintenance.

Since you've decided not to be one of these vehicle owners, the first step in working with your vehicle is simply learning more about it: the features, the kind of maintenance your make and model requires, and where you can find additional information to help you in your work. There are some notable differences between different vehicle types, although there are many similarities as well. For example, just about every vehicle needs oil, and this oil needs to be changed on a regular basis.

Hopefully, your check through the owner's manual and other resources covered in chapter 1 has given you a sense of the normal maintenance routines you need to follow for your vehicle.

Use the information found here to supplement what your manual tells you to do. Unlike your manual, this book provides step-by-step assistance.

REASONS TO MAINTAIN YOUR VEHICLE

There are a number of compelling and important reasons to perform regular maintenance on your vehicle. You might be surprised at how many of them aren't just aesthetic. They include the following:

- Increased safety—worn tires and wiper blades, malfunctioning brakes, leaking gas tanks, and exhaust buildups contribute to numerous accidents, injuries, illnesses, and deaths each year.
- Better performance—a vehicle whose oil and vital fluids are monitored and changed regularly is apt to keep performing well long after many poorly maintained vehicles begin to show signs of serious internal wear.
- Reduced pollution—vehicles are a huge contributor to global pollution, but a well-maintained car, truck, or SUV can limit the amount of noxious fumes pumped into the air and automotive fluids leaked into local water tables.
- Dependability—regular maintenance makes it much more likely your vehicle will be ready and able whenever you need to use it.
- Reduced cost of operation—along with dependability, regular maintenance tends to reduce your overall operating costs by limiting repairs caused by poor servicing and neglect and by keeping your fuel consumption reasonable well into the vehicle's life-span.
- Fewer emergencies—maintenance tasks like seasonal preparation diminish the likelihood you will be stranded with bad tires in a storm or have to cope with a cracked radiator during periods of extreme heat or cold.
- Better resale price—a well maintained vehicle usually fetches more money when you resell it as a used vehicle.

Of course, there is also the simple matter of pride of ownership. Even an older vehicle can continue to both look and operate like a much newer one if you maintain it properly. While we often underestimate the importance of having a good-looking and highly dependable car, it becomes a much bigger deal in a day and an age where every dollar counts, fuel is so expensive, and we may have to wait a few years more before we replace our current model.

So now let's move forward to what you can actually do about your vehicle maintenance yourself. Most maintenance steps are easy and inexpensive enough to remove all possible excuses for not keeping up with them. Factor in the time and money spent in trying to keep a poorly maintained vehicle on the road every day, and an outlay of resources once a month or every few months becomes much more reasonable.

MAINTENANCE STEPS

This section takes you through some of the most common and most vital maintenance procedures. From oil changes to flushing your radiator and replacing its coolant/water mix, you'll learn the process step by step.

Note that tune-ups, once considered part of basic maintenance, do not have to be performed as often as they did with older model vehicles. To learn more about the particular steps involved in a tune-up, turn to chapter 6.

Changing Oil

Regular oil changes should be considered a mandatory part of vehicle maintenance, since your car, truck, or SUV won't fare well if the oil volume is not kept at a proper level and you don't replace overworked lubricant with a fresh supply from time to time.

Your owner's manual should spell out how frequently you should change your oil; sometimes this is calculated in months but most frequently in miles (for example, every 3,000 to 4,000 miles). However, if you tend to use your car often for short trips rather than long ones, consider performing an oil change every four to six months. Whenever you change your oil, you should also change the oil filter.

Also in your owner's manual should be information about what grade of oil to use, which may vary by time of year. Once you know this information, you want to obtain:

- six quarts of the appropriate oil (at least five are usually used in the oil change while you can put the sixth quart in your trunk or storage area);
- an oil filter—look in your auto parts supply store or owner's manual for your make and model's oil filter type;
- one or more containers capable of holding up to six quarts of waste oil (consider buying one of the special oil containers that let you cover and store your waste oil rather than using a bucket that may spill); and
- a socket or combination wrench to remove the oil pan plug

You also may want to pick up what is frequently called an oil filter wrench, a tool used to help you replace the oil filter on your vehicle. It really depends on your filter type and car design whether this tool is really necessary; some people do oil changes regularly and have never used one, while others say this tool is priceless.

There is both regular vehicle oil and a synthetic form. Some manufacturers recommend using one or the other exclusively. Follow your manufacturer's suggestion. Many car experts go so far as to recommend that whatever type and brand of oil you use when you first buy the car should be the oil you use throughout the life of the vehicle. They believe that any mixing of brands or oil types is a bad idea.

When you're ready to do your oil change, make sure the engine is relatively cool. Then:

1. Locate the (usually hexagonal) plug on the oil pan underneath your car (see figure 5-1). Then check the height of your container and the ease with which you can remove the plug and slide the waste container into place. It may be necessary to jack your vehicle up to adequately drain your oil, but it's much safer if you can work without doing this.

2. Now go under your hood and locate and remove your oil fill cap (see figure 5-2), usually found near the dipstick you use to check your oil. Set the oil fill cap aside.

3. Go back under your car with both the waste oil container and the socket or combination wrench.

4. Place the container beneath the oil pan, centered under the plug.

5. Use your wrench to remove the oil pan plug. Set the plug aside.

6. Let the oil drain completely into the container. If you haven't brought your replacement oil to the car yet, do so now.

7. Once the oil is drained, go back beneath the vehicle, move the container gently out of the way, and use your socket/combination wrench to replace the oil pan plug.

8. Still under the car, locate the oil filter and then move the waste oil container beneath the filter.

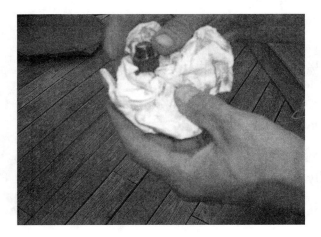

Fig. 5-1: Your owner's manual may diagram the location of your oil pan and its plug for easy reference. There is also likely a spot in the manual to record your oil changes so you can track when you last performed this maintenance routine.

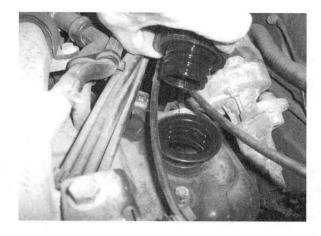

Fig. 5-2: The oil fill cap is located near the dipstick.

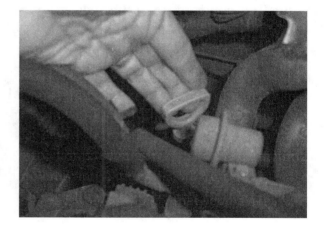

Fig. 5-3: When you check your oil dipstick, it's usually wise to draw the stick out as shown here, wipe it clean with a paper towel, reinsert the stick evenly, and then withdraw it again before you read the level.

9. Use your oil filter wrench to loosen and then remove your existing oil filter.
10. Get your fresh oil filter and, using a bit of oil from one of your replacement oil containers, coat the filter's rubber gasket thoroughly with lubricant. This step will help you loosen the filter the next time you do your oil change.
11. Go under the vehicle once more and, using the filter wrench, mount the new oil filter and tighten it between a quarter and a half turn.
12. Remove the waste container from beneath the car.
13. With your replacement oil, begin to fill the vehicle through the oil fill hole with five quarts (or whatever your owner's manual specifies).
14. Replace the oil fill cap.
15. Using your oil dipstick, check your oil level (see figure 5-3). At this point, the reading should show a high level because oil has not yet transferred into the new filter.

16. Cleaning any spilled oil from yourself first, start the vehicle and let it idle for about five minutes (don't rev the engine).
17. After five minutes, look beneath your vehicle for any sign of leakage. Should you see leaks, the filter or oil pan plug has not been replaced properly or securely, so fix this.
18. Turn off the engine and check the oil level again through the dipstick. Now it should read full.
19. Store your waste oil until you can dispose of it properly and clean your tools. You're done. You may want to record the date and your action in your car journal or in the appropriate spot in your owner's manual.

WARNING: Remember to check your vehicle's oil level at least once a week. If you see the oil light on your dashboard come on, don't ignore it. This could be due to a loose cap or plug, but you can't take the risk. Stop and check your oil level. Check for leaks. After all, it can take just a few miles of driving a car with little or no oil to destroy the engine.

Heating and Cooling System

Think beyond the matter of how comfortable the temperature is in your car. It's vital that you keep your engine running efficiently, never reaching excessively high operating temperatures that can lead to breakdown.

While a check of your heating and cooling system becomes particularly important when you're heading into the heat of summer or the subfreezing temperatures of winter, you should check this system routinely every time you do basic maintenance.

Flushing the Cooling System

Did you realize that the coolant in vehicle radiators breaks down over time and needs to be replaced? Once that breakdown happens, you inadvertently put a great deal of stress on the radiator and the entire rest of the car because the engine runs hotter. You can also see a buildup of both gunk (for lack of a better term) and mineral deposits that can reduce overall effectiveness.

How often you need to do this depends on your vehicle and weather conditions. In moderate climates, going through this procedure every year or two is usually satisfactory, while those living in areas with extreme heat—or cold—may need to do this before the start of every summer and winter. Consult your owner's manual for details.

You need to start with a cool engine. If you've been driving or otherwise running your vehicle, let it cool fully before you begin.

For this, you need:

- one or more containers or buckets in which to drain the current cooling fluid;
- fresh coolant; and
- radiator cleaning fluid (sometimes also called "coolant cleaning system")

Follow these steps:

1. With the engine off, open the hood.
2. Locate and release the radiator pressure cap (again, it's extremely important you start with a cool engine). Use extreme caution! (Note that whenever you need to remove the pressure cap when the car has been running, you must do it slowly to reduce the chance that pressure building up from behind the cap will send the cap and the radiator contents flying off when you begin to open it.)
3. Using your owner's manual or supplemental manual as a reference, get under the front of your vehicle and locate the valve or petcock that allows you to drain the radiator.
4. Position your drainage container under the valve or petcock to catch the draining fluid and then release the valve or open the petcock (see figure 5-4) and let the coolant drain fully.
5. When the radiator is completely empty, close the valve or petcock and remove the container or bucket.
6. Fill the radiator with plain water but do not—for the time being—replace the radiator cap.
7. Start the vehicle and let it idle while you add the coolant cleanser. The car may need to idle for 20 to 30 minutes or whatever time period is specified by the manufacturer of the coolant cleanser you buy for the job.

Fig. 5-4: Your radiator can be drained by releasing the valve or petcock located on the underside of the radiator. Be sure you have a container to catch the contents.

Savvy Tip

Try to find a container large enough to hold the contents of the radiator to use for draining your radiator. If you have to settle for a smaller container, be prepared to close the valve/petcock while you change out containers.

8. Turn off the engine and let it sit until it begins to cool.
9. Get a second container—or empty your first container into another receptacle until you can properly dispose of the fluid—and position it to catch the radiator's contents again.
10. Open the valve or petcock at the base of the radiator and let the radiator drain completely.
11. Close the radiator valve or petcock again and remove the filled bucket.
12. Fill the radiator with plain water again then start your engine and let it idle for about five minutes.
13. Once more, place a container beneath your radiator and open the valve/petcock to drain the contents before you close the valve/petcock. Then remove the container for the last time.
14. Follow directions on your antifreeze/coolant bottle and in your owner's manual. Usually, you need to fill your radiator with a 50-50 mix of water and coolant.
15. Be sure you replace the radiator cap.

WARNING: Coolant contains toxic fluid. Dispose of it properly and do not let pets or children anywhere near it while you work.

More Cooling/Heating System Cleanup

There are several more tasks you can perform periodically that will help keep your cooling and heating system working efficiently. Some of them are as simple as a cleanup, while others may involve replacement of hoses or caps.

First, look at the grille. If you're like most car owners and not very careful about keeping this clean, you'll note that the grille fills up with cobwebs, dead bugs, and just about anything else that might be flying through the air as you whiz along down the road.

Unfortunately, this stuff isn't just ugly and messy; it acts like a blanket that covers the front of the car, blocking the air circulation that helps the engine retain its heat. Thus, you want to clean this up from time to time to strip away the debris and let your car breathe some fresh, cool air.

Fig. 5-5: Notice the close quarters in which you have to work. For this reason, you may want to use a brush and a regular garden hose rather than a high-pressure washer.

Use a brush and your garden hose to clean out the grille area and remove the assorted debris you find there as shown in figure 5-5. I don't recommend using a pressure washer because the pressure spray could get out of control and you could end up damaging hoses or other parts.

Next, remove your radiator cap again—with the engine cool—and look at the seal around the cap. If it's badly worn or there's any cracking, you may want to buy a replacement radiator cap. Once the cap, which seals the radiator, begins to fail, the radiator itself can no longer function as efficiently as it should.

You should also clean out the cooling/heating vents inside your car. Dried leaves, dust, and other debris can collect in them, making it harder to push air through to cool or warm the passenger cabin. Every once in a while, turn your interior fan on high to blow dust and dirt out of the vents, preferably just before you vacuum out the car.

Some interior vents allow you to remove the exterior housing so you can vacuum them out. Consult your owner's manual for details.

Car Battery

Sure, many vehicle battery manufacturers advertise products that "require no maintenance whatsoever." In truth, however, at least a little care is required, including cleaning away all the grime and crud that can collect around your battery posts and clamps.

Some batteries require you to monitor one or more of their cells (see figure 5-6) to make certain there is enough water in place. To see if yours does, consult your owner's manual or the documentation that came with your last replacement battery. This should specify how you add water to the battery and what type of water. (Some will say tap water, others may tell you distilled water only.)

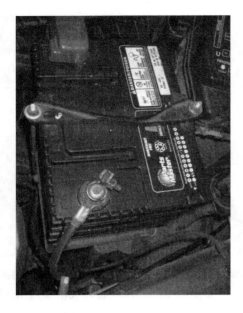

Fig. 5-6: While many batteries are sealed and require no maintenance, others require the addition of tap or distilled water to keep the battery running properly.

Grease and debris often collects around the battery. That's bad enough, but you can also have this material work its way between the battery headers and the terminals, fouling the connection.

Whenever you notice a buildup of material here, you should clean the car battery and its cables. To do so, follow these steps:

1. Following instructions likely found in your owner's manual, loosen the clamps holding the battery in place (see figure 5-7).
2. Make note of the connections so you can reattach the battery later.
3. Lift the battery out of the vehicle and place it on a clean, dry surface.
4. Make up a solution of water and baking soda (follow directions on the box for cleaning solution proportions) and locate a reasonably clean, stiff-bristled brush.
5. Use the brush (see the brush in figure 5-5) and your water–baking soda solution to thoroughly clean the top of the battery. Make certain the battery posts are free of debris.
6. Rinse the brush, apply more water–baking soda solution, and use the brush to clean the battery clamps.
7. When the battery and clamps are dry, replace the battery in the vehicle and reconnect it.

Checking and Changing Filters

There are filters beyond your oil filter that should be monitored and changed on a regular basis as spelled out in the owner's manual. These include:

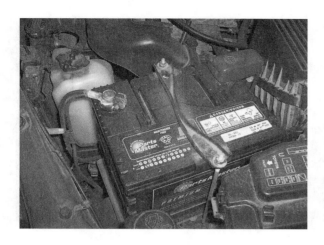

Fig. 5-7: Be sure to take note of the battery connections before you remove the battery from your vehicle. Also, take care not to yank the battery out; carefully loosen all connections first.

- air filter on top of the carburetor (often changed at tune-up time but usually should be changed more frequently);
- fuel filter; and
- PCV filter

Consult your manual for the fluid and filter replacements required and how frequently you need to perform these checks and changes.

Replacing Wiper Blades and Cleaning the Windshield Wells

You probably wouldn't believe how many accidents occur every year simply because a driver cannot see properly out of his or her windshield. While this can have several causes, including an inoperative defogging unit, the fault often lies with badly worn windshield wiper blades.

Good-quality wiper blades often don't need to be changed any more often than every year or two. Yet you should check the blades just about every time you do your routine maintenance, especially if you live in an area with frequent storms or conditions that often require you to use your wipers. See chapter 4 for instructions on changing wiper blades.

At the same time, you should clean any debris—including tree sap, dead bugs, grass, and dead leaves—from beneath the wiper blades and inside the windshield well, as described in chapter 4 (see figure 4-2). Material that comes up with the wiper blades from the windshield well can damage the wiper blades and even scratch the windshield glass.

Dirt and debris in the windshield can also block the spray of washer fluid. Sometimes, too, debris from this area can work its way down inside the vehicle where it can clog the washer fluid hoses or work its way into the air vents to blow the debris through the passenger compartment.

Fig. 5-8: Check your spare tire regularly for both inflation and tears or leaks, especially if you have a spare tire mounted outside the vehicle.

Other Things to Check Occasionally

These are the same things you have been told to check for before, but you need to remember to inspect them and do what is needed to bring them up to acceptable levels

- Tire pressure: Your owner's manual spells out the amount of pounds per square inch that are required for your size tires and your tires should neither be under- nor over-inflated; having an air compressor (see figure 4-4 for an example of a Delco air compressor) or even a quality bicycle pump on hand lets you inflate your tires as needed on the spot.
- Tire tread: You can pick up a tire gauge for just a few dollars that will help you determine when the tread is wearing thin so you can begin to plan your replacement; a gauge also helps you judge when parts of a tire are wearing more quickly than other parts.
- Use an old sheet or roll of butcher paper or leftover cheap wallpaper to place under your vehicle to check for leaks.
- Your spare tire: Make certain it's ready to go in case of an emergency (figure 5-8).
- Your jack: Be sure it's where it should be and that you can locate all the parts for it (see figure 5-9).
- Your in-car tool and emergency kit: It doesn't hurt to check this at least once every season and replace any "borrowed" or used components as needed.
- Hoses, belts, and cables: Whenever you're doing routine maintenance, take a good look at these (see figure 5-10) to try to locate and correct signs of wear; while you may be able to tape these up short-term, you probably want to replace a worn or damaged hose, belt, or cable as soon as possible.

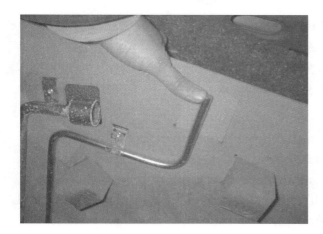

Fig. 5-9: Too many people discover they're missing part of their car jack only when they desperately need to use it to change a tire. Check the jack at least once a season.

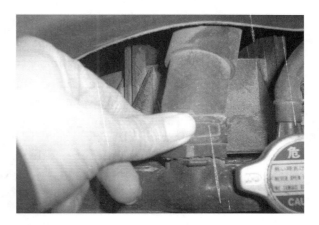

Fig. 5-10: Checking for signs of loose or damaged hoses, belts, or cables while your vehicle is sitting safely in your garage or driveway can save you from a nasty surprise when you're 20 miles from nowhere during a bad storm.

- Vehicle lights: As discussed in chapter 4, you should perform a regular check of all the lights in your vehicle, inside and out, and replace any bulbs (using replacement bulb types listed in your owner's manual) that have either failed or are no longer working fully or dependably.
- Your windows: Look for signs of cracks, chips, or trouble opening or closing side windows and replace any damaged windows as soon as possible. Also look at the seals around windows to make sure these are in good condition and then replace or repair as needed.

WARNING: Uneven tire wear may indicate one of several different problems: poor wheel alignment, under- or over-inflation of the tires, a badly worn vehicle suspension system, or issues with the vehicle's steering.

MAINTENANCE YOU SHOULD SCHEDULE

Unfortunately, not every maintenance routine for your vehicle is one you can easily do yourself. Here's a list of common maintenance procedures you should schedule with your dealership or local garage:

- Tire rotation and alignment: While you can change your own tires, as needed, it usually doesn't cost much to have that job done at the same time as the garage performs an alignment on your wheels to keep the car's movement steady and to keep tire wear even.
- Brake check: You can check your brake fluid and change small parts, but you still should have your entire brake system checked from time to time by a qualified professional who can spot deeper issues than you are apt to see yourself.
- Air conditioning: These systems are often fairly self-contained and usually require a qualified technician to inspect, clean, and replace parts.
- Transmission: Even if you aren't experiencing problems, you should have a mechanic check your transmission at least twice a year to try to catch small issues before they multiply or worsen. Since even small issues may require the removal of the engine, this isn't a job for weekend mechanics.

One last note, and yes, it brings us back to the issue of your owner's manual. Options you've added to your vehicle may require additional checks and maintenance beyond the types discussed in this chapter. Remember to check your manual thoroughly to catch any specifics and add them to your maintenance routine.

It also never hurts to have your garage or dealership go over a vehicle at least once a year even when you're doing your own maintenance. The mechanics there may spot something with their expert eyes that you haven't noticed. If your community or state requires annual car inspections, you may want to schedule that yearly garage trip just before your inspection date so they can check everything over to assure you of a passing grade.

6 TUNING IT UP!

- ◆ What's involved in a tune-up

- ◆ How often to tune up

- ◆ Identifying the symptoms of a poorly tuned vehicle

- ◆ Why you shouldn't wait for symptoms before you tune

- ◆ Understanding how computers can cause problems

- ◆ Performing a tune-up

An automotive tune-up, just as its name suggests, involves tweaking your vehicle and replacing some smaller parts and filters to help keep your car, truck, SUV, or minivan purring along efficiently. In this chapter, you'll learn what is involved in a standard tune-up and how much of the job—often 100 percent of it—you can do yourself without lots of fuss or muss.

But first, let's poke a hole in a common myth these days. If someone tells you that the vehicle tune-up is an outdated concept and something no one any longer needs to worry about, don't believe him.

While our vehicles have changed significantly in the past decade and some of those changes do affect the parts of the vehicle involved in a standard tune-up, most professionals will tell you that a tune-up is still an essential component of good automotive maintenance. The biggest change is that you simply don't have to perform a tune-up as frequently as in the past, when a tune-up every 30,000 miles was often recommended.

There is a big bonus that comes along with a tune-up that goes beyond just the continued good performance of your vehicle. In tuning our vehicles, we get up close and personal with what's under the hood. This makes it more likely we'll spot a loose or torn hose even if we aren't always faithful about performing regular inspections and routine maintenance. Also, the time you perform a tune-up happens to be an excellent time to take care of that inspection and maintenance.

WHAT'S A TUNE-UP?

Although different garages—and even different manufacturers—may define the steps involved in a classic vehicle tune-up in varying ways, there are some standard operations performed with a tune-up. These include the following:

- Checking and/or replacing the air filter, fuel filter(s), and PCV filter
- Replacing the spark plugs
- Inspecting the ignition points and replacing them if needed
- Checking and, if necessary, replacing the wires that run between the distributor cap and the cylinders where the spark plugs are installed
- Inspecting and cleaning the distributor cap and, if it's cracked or otherwise damaged, replacing it

THE WHY AND WHEN OF TUNE-UPS

Why do you need a tune-up? The reasons should be obvious and based on common sense: you want to keep your vehicle in top operating condition. Take the common example of a rough-running engine. Lots of pros will tell you that excessive idling generally isn't great for performance and overall car health. Manufacturers design vehicles to move, not to sit still. Unfortunately, with traffic almost everywhere becoming more congested with each passing year, more and more of us wind up spending at least as much time with our foot on the brake as on the gas pedal. This, in turn, can increase the need for more frequent tune-ups.

In fact, when a vehicle begins to operate with less power, get less gasoline mileage, or idle roughly or stall at stop signs and lights, a tune-up is the first thing many people think to do. A

Whenever you prepare to perform a tune-up, check the date and mileage since your last oil change. If it's been a while, consider killing two chickens with one car repair session. Chapter 5 tells you how to perform the oil change and install a fresh oil filter.

good mechanic or garage, however, will ask a customer why he or she wants the tune-up because the symptoms the vehicle is displaying might not be addressed by a tune-up. If your mechanic fails to ask, be sure to let him or her know anyway.

Many also think tune-up when it's time to have a vehicle inspected by a local or state vehicle safety or emissions program. However, many larger problems than those covered in a tune-up may be responsible when a vehicle fails an emissions inspection. You'll learn more about this at the end of the chapter.

HOW OFTEN TO TUNE YOUR VEHICLE

Your owner's manual should spell out exactly how often you should tune your vehicle. This is usually measured in miles (for example, every 40,000 or 60,000 miles) or months. Wherever possible, follow the recommendations provided and try not to go too long past the suggested tune-up period.

Some manufacturers also specify different recommended tune-up schedules that depend on whether your driving is mostly in the city, where you do a lot more stopping, starting, and just sitting in traffic, or on the highway where you're more apt to reach and sustain decent operating speeds.

Even if you're only halfway through a recommended tune-up period of 60,000 miles yet notice overall performance problems with the vehicle, there isn't any harm in going ahead and performing a tune-up. Unusual weather or driving conditions may have fouled your filter(s) and/or plugs and a tune-up may set things right.

WARNING: Some auto warranties mandate that you must perform a tune-up at least as frequently as the owner's manual recommends and that failure to do so may violate and invalidate the warranty. This is another good reason to familiarize yourself with your responsibilities—as well as the service company's—in regard to your warranty.

It's smart to increase your tune-up frequency whenever you're changing your driving habits. For example, if you usually just commute back and forth to work in your vehicle, but then find yourself driving much longer distances where the car is running for many hours at a time (or vice versa), the changes may tax the vehicle enough that tuning up more frequently is warranted.

SYMPTOMS OF A CAR OUT OF TUNE

If you've ever spent much time around a piano, you know it doesn't take an expert to figure out when that humungous musical instrument is out of tune. Hit an off key and that horrible sound will bounce around in your brain for a while.

While automobiles usually don't offer such dramatic evidence that it's time to tune, there are some common signs to alert you. These symptoms include the following:

- Stalling, hesitation, or pep that seems too pooped to pop
- Difficulty in starting and perhaps a little feedback when the engine is turned off (the latter can approximate the noise of a five-pack-a-day smoker on his first cough of the day)
- Engine runs more roughly, which is most noticeable when idling
- Knocking and pinging
- Exhaust that seems denser, more voluminous, and/or smells more pungent
- Decline in fuel efficiency

SAME SYMPTOMS, DIFFERENT CAUSES

While you just learned some of the most common symptoms of a vehicle in dire need of a tune-up, every one of these could be caused by something other than poor tuning or general neglect. Many of these symptoms, in fact, can spring from a wide variety of ills, as I've touched on before.

In this respect, an automobile's health can seem remarkably like our own. Say you go into the doctor complaining of a profoundly sour stomach. That funny tummy could be the result of anything from a reaction to last night's questionable leftovers to a condition as grave as cancer of the digestive system.

But a good doctor isn't going to immediately submit you to the thousands of dollars in tests necessary to evaluate every possibility. He or she is going to start with the most likely suspects and suggest you watch what you eat, maybe use an over-the-counter medication to calm your stomach, and call if you don't feel better in a few days.

Think of the tune-up as basic first-aid as well as preventive health care for your vehicle. Usually, a tune-up represents the least invasive, least expensive defense against the type of symptoms listed in "Symptoms of a Car Out of Tune." If after performing the tune-up you don't see improvement, then you can move on to other possible causes and solutions.

DON'T WAIT FOR SYMPTOMS

When money and time are tight—as they so often are—it's tempting to put off a regular vehicle tune-up. This may seem particularly attractive when your gas-driven workhorse doesn't have any of the nagging symptoms, discussed earlier, that are typically associated with a badly tuned auto.

But let me clue you in on why this is a temptation to resist even more assiduously than a 3 a.m. craving for a meal of cherry cheesecake and extra-large burritos. Our cars, trucks, and SUVs, just like our bodies, crave balance. Without that balance, a car or a human begins to run less efficiently. Over just a short period of time, that imbalance can lead to excessive wear and tear and opens the door to even bigger woes.

Dirty spark plugs in your vehicle, for example, not only represent an immediate issue but can lead to a fouled, badly performing engine. Wouldn't you prefer to shell out the dough for the spark plugs than for a major engine overhaul that could easily cost many hundreds of dollars? And consider the price of replacing an engine. A rebuilt one can run at least $1,500 and a brand new one substantially more.

EQUIPMENT YOU NEED FOR A TUNE-UP

At the very least, you will need the following parts:

- A replacement air filter
- Spark plugs, one per engine cylinder
- Spark plug gapping tool (when you replace the spark plugs, you need to set a designated amount of space or "gap" to allow air)
- Spark plug tool and usually a torque wrench

Savvy Tip

Some companies offer tune-up kits. This can be a great value, because a kit incorporates several needed replacement parts for a better price than buying each separately. But some kits are very limited, so you end up spending more to complete the package. Check and compare prices.

- Fuel filter (cleans fuel impurities as well as prevents the dirt that may be contained in your gas tank from getting into the engine; replacement is usually recommended every 30,000 to 40,000 miles or every few years)
- PCV filter, sometimes also called the PCV inlet filter (located in the air cleaner assembly very near the air filter), which should be changed whenever you replace the air filter and/or during a tune-up; a dirty or clogged PCV filter can severely impair engine performance)
- Clean cloths
- One or more smaller brushes appropriate for cleaning
- Compressed air, either from an air compressor or a can
- Masking tape and marker for labeling parts for reassembly

Beyond those items listed above, there are some additional possible hardware needs, such as:

- plug gaskets—you may need to replace the gaskets that may be found with your installed spark plugs;
- ignition wires/cables—if damaged or old, the wires or cables leading between your vehicle's distributor cap and spark plugs should be changed
- distributor cap—if cracked or otherwise damaged, replace this cap; and
- distributor ignition rotor—whenever you replace the distributor, you usually should replace the rotor that goes with it; some tune-up kits include both the cap and the rotor.

Note: Vehicles manufactured in 1980 or earlier may require additional checks as part of a tune-up. For example, you may need to replace ignition points, as spelled out in your owner's manual.

BEFORE YOU DO IT YOURSELF

Before you get started doing a tune-up and even before you decide whether you can or should do it yourself, there's a bit of information you should consider first.

First, the time it takes to perform a tune-up can really vary between make and model of vehicle as well as in the condition of each vehicle. For example, a poorly maintained car that hasn't benefited from regular tune-ups may take at least a few hours more than a vehicle that has had good and consistent care, simply because cleaning and inspecting parts takes time. A big-engine vehicle like an SUV or van also may have more spark plugs and parts to check than a compact model car, so each step requires more time and effort.

On average, even a minimal tune-up on a well-maintained vehicle will take more than an hour. On average, you should plan for at least three to five hours of your time to complete an adequate tune-up if you plan to roll an oil change and an overall vehicle inspection into the job. Often, mechanics plan for two to four hours and they're the pros with far more experience performing tune-ups than you.

Before you decide whether to go the do-it-yourself or the garage route, determine whether:

- you have the time (if you're in reasonably good health, you should have enough physical stamina to do the work);
- you have the information needed—your owner's manual should spell out exactly what types of plugs, air filter, and other replacement components you need, right down to the spark plug gap you need to set; if you can't find the information in the manual, buy a Chilton's, Haynes, or other manual or ask your auto parts store for assistance in getting what you need;
- it would be more cost effective to have a garage do it—some garages offer special deals on tune-ups to attract new customers who may use the garage again for more expensive repairs—but make sure you know what the garage checks and replaces in a tune-up and price the individual parts at your auto supply store so you can figure out the costs involved in doing it yourself

DOING YOUR TUNE-UP

Now that you've researched the exact parts you need and pulled your equipment together, it's time to get down to the nitty-gritty. And yes, a tune-up tends to be a dirty job, largely because you'll be removing a lot of the dirt, grease, and carbonized debris that tends to clog up filters and plugs and various parts. Dress accordingly and don't feel like a sissy if you decide to wear gloves for this job.

First, you want to start with a cool engine. Since you'll be handing a number of parts under the hood, you don't want these components to be too hot to tolerate. If you're planning to perform other routine maintenance like a full self-inspection or oil change during the session, you may

> ### THE COMPUTERIZED AUTO AND THE TUNE-UP PROCESS
>
> Today's more computerized automobiles have been painstakingly designed to try to keep their motors running as efficiently as possible for as long as possible. One chief way the onboard computer does this is to make adjustments on the fly to compensate for certain problems it detects (for example, correcting for an iffy air-fuel mix). Clearly, this does us a big favor compared with older models because we don't have to pop the hood as often to play around or call a mechanic to do the same.
>
> Yet there's always a price attached to convenience. In this case, these computerized controls also act to camouflage problems that would otherwise alert you to the vehicle's need for corrective care. Some models do such a bang-up job of quick fixes that you may not have any idea anything is wrong until the vehicle stops working. Once the computer has run out of tricks, it may just give up.
>
> If this sounds a little like your home computer, it should. PCs and their operating systems also perform a fair amount of behind-the-scenes corrections to try to keep the system running—at least until it quits.

want to accomplish those tasks first, remembering to refer to chapters 3 and 4 on inspection and chapter 5 on basic maintenance.

Now the exact order in which you perform the various parts of the tune-up usually doesn't matter unless your owner's manual specifies certain tasks be done first. Here, let's start with replacing the necessary filters.

Replacing Your Filters

Because the primary job of any filter is to prevent unwanted materials from getting into the operating equipment, a filter can often become hopelessly clogged with dirt and debris. Sometimes this can be cleaned out so you can continue to use the filter for at least a short period of time. Normally, however, you want to replace such filters on a regular basis, such as at the time of a tune-up.

There are three major filters typically inspected and replaced during a tune-up: the air filter, the PCV filter, and the fuel filter. Let's take each in order.

Access to the PCV filter may be found in the same general location as the air filter. So you may want to try to locate this filter and replace the PCV filter (covered in the next section) at the same time you perform the air filter replacement so you don't have to remove the filter cover again or otherwise go to extra work.

Changing Your Air Filter

Think of the air filter as the protection for the "lungs" of your vehicle. If the filter is clean and in good shape, it should do a superb job of preventing dirt, dust, and debris from getting into the fuel system where it can wreak havoc.

Be a savvy vehicle owner by replacing your air filter with every tune-up. However, you may need to replace the air filter more often than you perform a tune-up; some mechanics recommend this filter be replaced every 15,000 to 20,000 miles.

Thankfully, this is one of the simpler operations you can perform. At the same time, it also can make a huge difference in maintaining satisfactory car performance and prevention of problems that can lead up to some of the most expensive and extensive repairs.

Check your owner's manual for the replacement filter type you need to buy. If you can't locate specifics, don't worry; your auto parts store will have a way you—or they—can look up the filter type needed for your make and model. You usually can choose between your vehicle manufacturer's replacements and less expensive third-party manufacturer filters that often can be just as good as the costlier "official" versions.

To replace your air filter:

1. With the car hood open, locate the covering for your air filter, usually found near the center at the top of the engine. A clip or a screw may hold the cover in place. Remove the cover (see figure 6-1) and set it aside. On some vehicles, the air filter and its cover may actually be mounted near one of the fenders under the hood and may require that you disconnect the air intake hose from the cover before you can pull off the cover.
2. Lift out the existing air filter, trying not to shake it or loosen the dust and debris.
3. Using compressed air and/or a cloth, clean the area where the former air filter sat. Doing this prevents the new filter from becoming dirty too quickly.
4. Install the new filter.
4. Replace the cover and secure the cover in place.

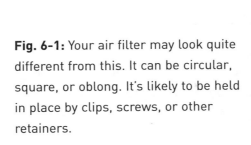

Fig. 6-1: Your air filter may look quite different from this. It can be circular, square, or oblong. It's likely to be held in place by clips, screws, or other retainers.

Spot-Checking the Air Filter

If you experience problems starting your vehicle or with proper idling between tune-ups, don't be afraid to go under the hood and check the condition of the air cleaner. Depending on your road conditions and the overall shape of your vehicle, it's possible you may need to replace the air filter more often than just every time you tune up.

Look at the filter. Note that there is a center ring of folded paper or paper-like material that actually serves as the dirt trap. You want to get as much of the dirt and dust out of here as possible without damaging the filter housing.

Here's another tip if you notice the air filter is dirty but you don't have a replacement filter right on hand. Take the air filter to a large wastebasket and tap it to try to loosen and remove dust and debris.

Normally, you should not run water over the filter or apply any solvents to clean it. Just removing loosened dirt may be enough to get you through until you can get a replacement—so long as you don't procrastinate for several months.

However, if the air filter appears in very poor shape—the screening over the filter itself is separating or there is still a significant amount of dirt in place once you shake it out—replace it ASAP.

Removing and Replacing Your PCV Filter

PCV is a much shorter way of saying "positive crankcase ventilation." The PCV filter prevents dirt and debris from making its way into your PCV valve. This valve plays a major role in filtering out nasty gasses produced by very hot oil before they can be passed into the air cleaner, which would literally foul up the works.

Unfortunately, the PCV filter isn't always as easy to find as the larger and more distinctive air filter. Consult your owner's manual along with any other documentation you may have, including a Chilton's, Haynes, or other manual, to try to locate it. The valve—and its filter—is usually found where the return hose from the air cleaner meets the valve cover.

Swapping Out the Fuel Filter(s)

A vehicle performs best when its fuel supply is kept as free of dirt and other contaminants as possible. Any unwanted material in the fuel—even flakes of rust and dirt that make it into the fuel tank—can have a big and unpleasant effect on the way a vehicle operates. The fuel filter serves to screen out dirt and impurities before the gas mix enters your engine.

Like the air filter, the fuel filter(s) may need to be checked and replaced more frequently than recent model vehicles require a tune-up. Between 15,000 and 30,000 miles is a good interval to replace the fuel filter(s). Also, if you're not sure of your fuel source—for example, you don't know if the filling station you use has good, clean storage tanks—you may want to reduce the length of time between filter checks and replacements.

While many vehicles have just a single fuel filter, some makes and models have two or more. Check your owner's manual to make sure you can identify any additional filter and filter locations before you begin.

WARNING: Since a fuel filter is apt to be full of fuel residue, do not smoke around it or have anything capable of producing a flame close by. As you remove the existing fuel filter(s), dispose of it carefully so that the fuel cannot leak into the ground or onto other material or parts.

Your first task is to locate your fuel filter. If your owner's or other manual does not make its position clear, the best thing to do is to locate the fuel line, a sturdy but pliant thick finger-width hose that comes up from the gas tank usually found at the bottom rear of your vehicle, and follow that line up to the engine under the hood. The fuel filter(s) usually lies at the end of the fuel line just as it enters the engine at or near the carburetor. A clamp typically holds the fuel filter to the fuel line.

One problem you face is that your fuel line, even with the engine cold, is going to contain some fuel. So you have to be prepared to block the escape of fuel by plugging the end of the fuel line so you can replace the fuel filter. Actually, you will have to provide two stopgaps, because there is an additional hose between the fuel filter and the engine itself that also must be plugged. Pencils, tubes, or small stoppers of the exact right size can be pressed into service for this, but have this in place before you start or you'll have gas everywhere, presenting a fire hazard and more.

When ready, follow these steps:

1. Use a screwdriver to loosen the clamp holding the filter to the fuel line.
2. Stop the fuel line so no gas escapes.
3. Identify how the fuel filter is held in place. On many vehicles, two small bolts secure this to the engine. Use whatever tool fits the situation to remove these retainers and set them aside where you can find them later.
4. Determine how the current fuel filter is installed. You'll want to match this as you install the replacement.
5. Block the hose running from the filter to the engine.
6. Remove the existing fuel filter and dispose of it properly. Your auto parts store or local recycling center may have a way for you to get rid of this which is better than throwing it in the landfill.
7. Insert the new filter and secure it in place.
8. Carefully remove the stop from the first blocked hose and reattach it, then do the same for the other hose.
9. Resecure the clamp or clip that holds the hose(s) to the filter.
10. Look to be sure that the hoses are attached securely and that there is no leak.
11. Clean up thoroughly, since you likely have gas on your skin and/or your shirt cuffs or gloves.

Nice work! With the filters changed out, you can move on to replacing your spark plugs and checking the distributor cap for signs of wear, tear, or burning.

Changing Your Spark Plugs

First and foremost, you want to be sure you use the exact type and number of spark plugs for your vehicle as recommended in your owner's manual. Normally for a tune-up, you replace all spark plugs at the same time.

Next, you want to have your masking tape and a marking pen available. As you remove the ignition wires or cables that connect the spark plugs and the cylinders they're installed into to the distributor cap, you want to label each wire with the spark plug/cylinder it came from, as shown in figure 6-2.

Fig. 6-2: Using masking tape and your pen, label each wire so you know which spark plug/cylinder it goes to. This makes it a breeze to reinstall the wires once you've inserted the new spark plugs.

Here's the process:

1. With the ignition wires labeled, begin to remove them one by one from the spark plug. Place your fingers around the boot of the wire near the spark plug and then lift. Do not yank on the wires to remove them.

2. Use a spark plug socket wrench to remove the spark plugs one by one (see the sidebar "Spot-Checking Individual Spark Plugs" to learn what to do if you see particular damage to one or more spark plugs you remove).

3. Use compressed air to remove dirt or buildup around each of the cylinder openings where the spark plugs were removed; try not to blow the dirt into the cylinder.

4. Remove the new spark plugs from their packaging.

5. Use a spark plug gapping tool and instructions from your owner's manual to set the recommended gap size at the business end of each spark plug.

6. Check your owner's manual again to see if it recommends using anti-seize compound to the spark plugs before you replace them. If so, obtain this compound and apply it according to directions.

7. Install each spark plug by screwing it into place and tightening it by hand. Make sure they are firmly and fully seated.

8. Tighten each plug using a torque wrench (see figure 6-3) (your owner's manual may also suggest a different tool). Take care that you do not cross-thread the spark plugs as you install them and that you do not overtighten them.

9. Replace the ignition wires using the labels you applied as a guide to determine which wire corresponds to which plug. Again, double check the seating to ensure that each is secure.

Fig. 6-3: A torque wrench is the tool needed to tighten spark plugs. But be very careful not to strip the threads on plugs or inside the cylinder or to overtighten the plugs.

Fig. 6-4: The distributor cap is located at the end of the ignition wires leading from the spark plugs. There are variations in cap type that require slightly different removal and replacement methods.

Inspecting Your Distributor Cap and Rotor

The distributor cap (see figure 6-4) is usually fairly simple to locate because it's at the other end of the ignition wires connected to the spark plugs. This cap serves as the cover to the ignition system distributor. A tune-up does not always include the replacement of the distributor cap and its associated rotor, but these components should be inspected and, if needed (and it usually is), cleaned at the time of the tune-up.

Because it's an integral part of the system that starts the car and carries voltage, the distributor cap can become damaged. Evidence of damage can include a burned appearance or carbon buildup on, around, or under the cap. To see this, you usually need to remove the distributor cap, although some types of injury—like a broken terminal where the ignition wires come into the top of the cap—can be seen with the cap in place.

A cap that is cracked, broken, or shows fire damage must be replaced. A vehicle without a distributor cap won't turn over; a vehicle with a damaged distributor cap won't start easily. A very dirty distributor cap should be thoroughly cleaned; if it resists complete cleaning, it should be replaced as soon as possible.

SPOT-CHECKING INDIVIDUAL SPARK PLUGS

While it's smart to replace all spark plugs at the time you perform a tune-up, you may want to go back and look at individual spark plugs again later if you experience a problem with getting the vehicle to start. A fouled spark plug can be the cause of starting failure.

To do this, you simply remove one spark plug at a time, following the same basic steps you used in spark plug replacement. As you go, check each spark plug to see if there are signs of excessive wear, damage, or dirt. Any dirt should be thoroughly removed using a clean cloth and/or compressed air before you reinstall the plug.

If, in your spot inspection, you notice that one or more spark plugs, although relatively new, appear very badly worn or even distorted, replace all such plugs with new ones. Make note, however, of which cylinders these damaged plugs were installed to and then make an appointment with your mechanic or local garage. Take the damaged plugs with you when you take the vehicle in.

Excessive damage or distortion of a spark plug may be a sign of a serious engine problem. This should be examined by a professional with the equipment and experience to troubleshoot the issue and make repairs, if necessary.

Even if there is no obvious damage to the outer part of the cap, remove the cap to inspect inside it and clean it. Depending on the distributor cap type your vehicle has, there are different ways to remove the cap. Normally, the cap should be removed with the ignition wires leading to the spark plugs still attached, even if you expect to replace the distributor cap as part of the process (you'll see why later in this section).

Do not try to remove the distributor cap by yanking on the ignition wires. This can damage the distributor cap or the wires, or both. For caps with screws, remove the (usually two) screws, set them aside, and then gently but firmly remove the cap itself. For lock-style caps, push down on the cap, turn, and then lift the cap up. For spring-loaded caps with a clip, disengage the clips and then remove the cap.

With the distributor cap off the distributor, look inside for any signs of damage or wear. You should be able to see at least one small vent on the cap; be sure this is clear of debris and not clogged. Use a small brush to remove deposits of carbon and dirt that may be found inside, using care not to damage the cap or its structures.

Remember how you removed the distributor cap because you will follow the same steps in reverse to replace it or install a new cap.

WARNING: Although it may be tempting to use a strong solvent or even compressed air to try to remove recalcitrant dirt or carbon, avoid both. Your auto supply store may sell a special small, roundhead brush that can make the job of cleanup of the cap easier.

If the distributor isn't in good condition or can't be cleaned, you must replace it. Usually, you replace the rotor assembly at the same time you install the new distributor cap. Many tune-up kits and distributor kits include both a rotor and a distributor cap.

If your existing cap is fine and you've cleaned it, replace it on the distributor, making certain it is firmly seated and secure.

Now let's look at how to replace a distributor cap if that is necessary. Notice that when you removed the cap, you were advised to keep the wires attached. The logic here is that if you need to replace the cap, you can use the placement of the existing wires to understand how to transfer those wires to the right terminals on the new cap. You will take each wire off, one at a time, and attach it to the replacement cap. Here's what to do:

1. Place the new cap securely on the distributor.
2. Use the existing distributor cap as a guide and remove the first of the spark plug ignition wires from that cap to install on the replacement. Continue until all the wires are in place, and both correctly and firmly seated.

When a Tune-Up Doesn't Fix Your Vehicle's Performance

Remember what you read earlier in this chapter: if your vehicle's overall operation and performance seems to be heading south, a tune-up is a cost-effective and fairly simple way to check, maintain, and replace components that may affect drivability and performance. But a tune-up by itself may not completely fix the situation.

If you perform your own tune-up but still encounter rough idling, bad fuel consumption, or excessive exhaust, you may want to invest some of the dollars saved into a more thorough check by a professional mechanic. Let the mechanic know what you did as part of the tune-up so he or she won't replace parts you've just changed out—unless, of course, the mechanic happens to find that you didn't use the correct part or didn't install it properly.

A more thorough check may involve the following:

- Inspection and testing of the oxygen sensor: A failing oxygen or air sensor can increase your fuel consumption by as much as 20 percent in a very short time while also producing rather rough running.
- PCV valve replacement: The PCV valves themselves, which the PCV filter covers, may need to be cleaned and/or replaced; persistent and otherwise unexplained higher-than usual oil consumption and/or oil leaks are a common indicator of PCV valve trouble.
- Carburetor inspection: A fouled carburetor is a frequent source of problems when your symptoms include reduced fuel efficiency, rough idling, and increased and foul-smelling exhaust; sometimes, replacement is necessary, but you can usually save some money if you purchase a rebuilt carburetor with a warranty.

WHAT TO DO IF YOUR VEHICLE FAILS AN EMISSIONS TEST

Many states and even foreign countries require periodic vehicle inspections that frequently include an emissions test to be sure a vehicle isn't producing unusually high levels of noxious fumes that can contribute to air pollution and even to global warming.

A simple tune-up like that recommended in this chapter can often bring a vehicle's emissions under control enough to pass a standard emissions inspection. It's often smart to perform a tune-up before you go in for the inspection to increase the chances you'll pass on the first try.

However, more serious underlying problems with a vehicle that a standard tune-up won't address can also cause an emissions test failure. A fouled or damaged carburetor, PCV valves in need of replacement, issues that result from a failure to change oil regularly, and a badly worn engine are just some of the causes. Additional culprits include a fuel-injected vehicle in dire need of an air/fuel adjustment or complete overhaul, valves or valve gaskets that need adjustment or replacement, and a clogged or malfunctioning choke (automatically controlled on most vehicles today).

If your vehicle has had a full tune-up and yet fails the emissions part of the exam, have the vehicle thoroughly checked out by a good mechanic. Keep in mind that you don't simply need to pass the test; you need to perform any repairs needed to maintain the vehicle in, or return it to, dependable running condition.

7 COPING WITH THE TOP 10 COMMON PROBLEMS, PART 1

◆ Curing poorly behaved car alarms

◆ Replacing a dark headlight and more

◆ Dealing with a soft or flat tire

◆ Raising a battery from the dead, from jump-starting through replacement

◆ Tightening a loose fan belt and replacing a broken one

By now, you've already had quite a bit of hands-on experience inspecting, maintaining, and even repairing your vehicle. You've coped with rust, performed an oil change and a tune-up, and flushed your radiator. Through it all, you've checked and replaced fluids and swapped out filters.

In this chapter and the one that follows, you're moving up to tackle 10 of the most common problems that tend to afflict us as the owners and operators of a vehicle. Here, you'll deal with some of the easier ones, including curing an annoying car alarm, installing a replacement headlight, and recharging and/or replacing a battery. You'll also learn how to check, tighten, and even replace the all-important fan belt.

Then, in chapter 8, you take on the tougher jobs like overcoming problems with a vehicle that won't start or is burning far more fuel than it used to consume.

FIXING A MALFUNCTIONING CAR ALARM

A malfunctioning car alarm isn't just an incredible annoyance. The lights and sound produced by the alarm can quickly drain your battery. In some communities, misbehaving alarms can also subject the owner to tickets for disturbing the peace.

We've all come across vehicles in a parking lot where the alarms sound at the least provocation, even the slam of the door on an adjacent car or someone brushing against the "armed" vehicle while walking through the lot. The same thing happens on the streets every day.

Your best bet with a problem car alarm is first to read through any documentation that came with the alarm to see what it recommends, and to make certain the remote device you use to control it (see figure 7-1) has a fresh battery and is functioning well. Many alarms display a flash of light to indicate when you turn them on or off, while others send audio cues. If the remote does not work, be sure there is nothing obstructing the radio wave transmission between the remote and the alarm, like something you may have added to the vehicle since you got the alarm. Some remotes are extremely fussy and demand you point them at a specific location like one or more sensors positioned on the vehicle. If you don't aim right for that spot, you can press the button all you want and you won't get anywhere.

If you cannot find anything else wrong and the documentation does not provide much detail, you need to have the alarm serviced, preferably by whoever installed it in the first place. They can adjust the sensitivity of the alarm so it is less apt to be triggered by simple things in the environment.

If you can't get an immediate appointment, you might want to consider temporarily disarming the alarm. How you do this can vary by alarm type and may involve

Fig. 7-1: Your vehicle alarm remote may need to be in direct alignment with the signal itself to turn off the alarm. If the remote fails to work, try replacing its battery and making certain nothing is in the way of the signal between the remote and the alarm.

Sometimes, something as minor as a bit of dirt or dried liquid on the signal part of the remote or the vehicle sensor itself can block the signal. Use a dry wipe to clean the remote and sensor.

- simply not turning on the alarm;
- turning off a switch on the alarm console; or
- removing the vehicle fuse that arms the alarm.

But if you live in a high-crime area, you may not want to disarm the alarm even temporarily. Until you can get an appointment to fix the alarm, try to park the vehicle in a location where it is less likely to be brushed against or jostled.

REPLACING A DARK HEADLIGHT AND TURN SIGNAL LIGHT

Headlights

Don't let a headlight stay dark once it goes out. Not only does it make it harder for you to see when driving at night, which can affect your safety, it's also a common reason for a police stop, which may result in a ticket. While replacement is usually a bit more time consuming than changing a light bulb in your home, it's easily doable with the right parts and a bit of patience.

First, be sure you know which headlight is out. Simply turn on your headlights and check. At the same time, check the other headlight that is not out. If you notice it's dimmer than it should be, you may want to go ahead and replace both headlights at the same time, since it may be only a matter of weeks before the other one fails.

Next, check your owner's manual. This should tell you not only what type of replacement headlight you need, but also whether you can simply replace the lamp or bulb itself or whether you need to buy a whole new assembly. Your local auto parts store can also help you determine this.

Once you have your replacement bulb or full headlight, here are the usual steps to take to replace it, depending on whether you need to just substitute the bulb or the full headlight.

To replace the full headlight:

1. Open your hood, since most headlights are accessed through the very front of the engine compartment.

Make your driving experience and that of other drivers easier by not using a different headlight type to replace a single dead headlight. For example, if you replace a standard light with a single high-power halogen headlight, you create an imbalance in the area of light in front of your vehicle. This can make it more difficult for you to see and drivers of oncoming vehicles may be distracted by one extremely bright light and one duller one.

2. Using your owner's manual as the guide, locate your headlight assembly in the vehicle.

3. Remove any nuts, screws, or retainers. Place these in a safe place so you can locate them again quickly. An empty can or cup works well for this purpose.

4. Pull out the headlight assembly. If necessary, unplug it from any wires coming into it. Dispose of the headlight properly (halogen headlights should not be placed in the regular trash but disposed of at your auto parts store or local recycling center or hazardous waste pickup).

5. Install the new headlight and plug any wires you remove from the old headlight assembly into the new one.

6. Replace any screws, nuts, or retainers.

7. Close the hood.

To replace the bulb only:

1. Open your hood.

2. Locate the headlight assembly.

3. Twist to remove the black plastic ring that holds the bulb in the assembly (see figure 7-2).

4. Pull the bulb and its housing out.

5. Remove the bulb from its housing.

6. Take the replacement bulb from its packaging, exercising care not to touch the glass itself (this is particularly important with halogen-type bulbs).

7. Insert the new bulb in its housing.

8. Slide the bulb assembly back into the headlight.

9. Tighten the black plastic ring again.

10. Close the hood.

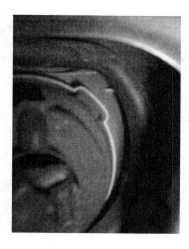

Fig. 7-2: A black plastic ring often holds the bulb assembly in place. Twisting it will allow you to remove the bulb assembly and replace the bulb.

Turn Signal Indicator Light

Now that you've handled a headlight replacement—usually the biggest light job on the vehicle—the rest should be easier. Let's replace a burned out turn signal indicator light.

Follow these steps:

1. Check your owner's manual to determine whether you can access the bulb from the outside by removing screws or clips that hold the light cover in place, or from inside the vehicle such as under the hood or the trunk, much like you did with the headlight.
2. Get a replacement bulb of the proper type as spelled out in your owner's manual.
3. Open the light assembly. For some, you need to open the hood if it's a front indicator light or the trunk if it's a rear light and remove screws or retainers holding the light assembly in place; for others, you remove screws or clips from the outside and then pull the cover off to get at the bulb.
4. Unscrew the existing bulb.
5. Install the replacement bulb.
6. Replace the cover or light assembly, replace any screws, clips, or other retainers, and shut the trunk lid or hood.

Voila! You're done. Congratulations!

Savvy Tip

It doesn't hurt to go to the extra trouble of cleaning your headlights and other lights when you replace a bulb. Something as simple as dust and mud deposits can considerably reduce light visibility.

If you recently purchased your tires, they may be under warranty and thus covered for any problems that occur within the coverage period. Check your bill or documentation from your tire replacement to see if this applies.

DEALING WITH A SOFT OR FLAT TIRE

At one time or another, you are going to face a tire that is either getting soft or goes flat while you're driving.

Follow the advice in earlier chapters for checking your tire and tire pressure as part of routine maintenance and you are far less likely to be hit with the nasty surprise of a flat tire while out on the road. Yet there is always the possibility that glass or something else sharp may puncture the tire or that a long, hot drive may exacerbate a defect in the tire, making it go flat.

When the Tire Goes Soft at Home

If you are at home when you see or experience a flat or very soft tire, your first step should be to add air to the tire to return it to normal. However, you also want to look at the tire for any signs of puncture or other damage. If you see something sharp like a piece of glass or nail embedded in the tire, remove it carefully. Once you add air, wait to see if the tire goes soft again in a short period of time. If so, add air again and then move your hand around the tire (see figure 7-3) to see if you can feel air coming out, thus indicating the location of problem. It may be possible to have your local garage patch the tire, and you may be able to use a flat-fixing solution to keep the tire inflated long enough to reach a garage.

Fig. 7-3: Add air to the tire and then move your hand over various parts of the tire to see if you can determine the location of the leak or weak spot. You may be able to get the tire patched rather than having to replace it.

WHAT TO KNOW ABOUT FLAT-TIRE SPRAY REMEDIES

The technical editor for this book, Richard White, reminds us of some very important information about your use of emergency flat tire sprays. If you take a tire in for repair after you apply this spray, be sure to tell your auto technician about it.

For one, the contents of these sprays are flammable. It's wise to alert anyone when a flammable substance is present that they may not know about.

Beyond that, however, more than a few technicians have been treated to a spray of this substance as they begin to work on the tire. This not only creates a mess but can be dangerous since this material can be irritating or worse if it gets into the eyes or is inhaled.

When the Tire Goes Flat on the Road

If you are in motion at the time you feel something go wrong with the tire, pull over to the side as quickly as possible. You want to be completely off the road, with room to walk around the vehicle and to work so you don't risk being hit by another vehicle. Wherever possible, you want to pull off into a fairly level spot with stable ground or pavement beneath you in case you need to change the tire.

Once you check the tire, if you see that it is flat or nearly so, you should:

1. Turn on your hazard lights.
2. Remove the flares or other emergency lights from your in-vehicle emergency kit and set them up. These will alert other drivers you have a problem.
3. Check your spare tire and make certain you have your complete vehicle jack assembly, if needed.

If you followed my advice to have a can of tire-inflation material in your vehicle, you may be able to use this to restore the tire long enough to either get home or to a garage for a proper repair. This is usually a better option than having to use the jack to raise the car and replace the tire by the side of the road.

Follow the directions on the can to apply the flat-tire-fix solution, such as Fix-A-Flat. With some, you may need to use the entire container. Plan to replace the Fix-A-Flat can as soon as possible in case you need it again.

WARNING: Do not try to drive long distances using just the Fix-A-Flat spray. You really need to get home or to a garage as quickly as possible or the tire may go flat again.

Replacing Your Tire with a Spare

Too many people have no idea of how to change a tire—and that applies to men as well as to women. Yet there are times when the Fix-A-Flat solution does not work—such as when the damage to the tire is severe—and you need to swap out the existing tire with your spare before you can get somewhere else for assistance.

Before you do this, understand that using a jack is serious business. People can get badly hurt by not exercising extreme caution when propping up the vehicle. You want as flat and level a surface as possible and you want to be sure that as you seat the jack on the ground you have a firm purchase on it. Follow directions in your owner's manual for using the jack before you attempt to use it.

Also, if you haven't followed earlier advice to regularly inspect your spare tire to make certain it's ready in case of emergency, check it before you try to put it to use. You don't want to go to all the trouble of jacking up the vehicle only to discover that your spare is actually an old tire with damage that you forgot to replace.

Then:

1. Use an old cloth to remove excess dirt or debris from the tire and wheel.
2. Remove the spare tire from your vehicle. It's better to do this before the car is jacked up so you don't have to jostle the vehicle removing it later.
3. Locate your jack and all its components (see figure 7-4) and remove them from the vehicle.
4. If your wheel has a wheel cover/hubcap, remove it.

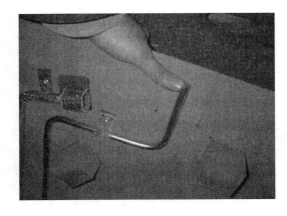

Fig. 7-4: Make sure you have all the parts needed for your jack and remove them all from the vehicle before you start to work.

Fig. 7-5: Always use extreme care when using the jack. Keep children and pets away from the vehicle and keep all parts of your anatomy from the underside of the vehicle as you work. Do not forget to consult the owner's manual.

5. Using the lug device that usually comes with the jack, loosen the lug nuts on the bad tire before jacking up the car.

6. Read your owner's manual to determine how to use the jack.

7. Following the directions in the owner's manual, place the jack below the bumper at the front or back of the vehicle, wherever your flat is located.

8. Use the jack handle (as shown in figure 7-5) to raise the vehicle just high enough to take the weight off the flat tire and allow its removal and replacement. Do not jack the vehicle up as high as the jack will go.

9. Remove the lug nuts and set them aside.

10. Pull the bad tire off, using extreme care not to jostle the vehicle or allow your body to get under the wheel well in case the jack slips. Set the bad tire aside for the time being.

11. Mount your spare tire in the bad tire's place.

12. Screw on the lug nuts but don't tighten them—you will tighten them after the car is off the jack.

13. Again following directions in the owner's manual, slowly and carefully lower the vehicle back to the ground.

14. Remove the jack and disassemble it.

15. Use the tire bar or lug device to secure the lug nuts, making them as tight as you can get them.

16. Replace the jack in its proper place and put the bad tire in the space formerly occupied by the spare.

17. Turn off your hazard lights and remove any emergency lights you have set out.

After you replace the tire, be careful as you drive. Do not travel at excessive speeds and be sensitive to any wobble or shimmy in the wheel, which may indicate the lug nuts on the tire you changed are working their way loose. If so, pull the vehicle over and retighten the nuts.

Your very next step should be to visit a garage to check and, if needed, add pressure to the spare tire. Also check the tightness of the lug nuts you replaced. You also may want to drop off the damaged tire to see if it can be repaired so it can become your new spare.

WARNING: Never have anyone in the vehicle when you jack it up; this includes small children. Also, do not try to access the vehicle interior while the jack is in place. If you absolutely must get something inside the car after you raise it with the jack, disengage the jack before you so much as open the car door.

Recharging or Replacing a Dead Battery

Most batteries are designed to last at least five years. However, many different factors come into play that can affect the life of the battery such as

- poor maintenance;
- other vehicle problems that may demand more from the battery, including a failing alternator;
- corrosion to battery cables and posts that can ultimately damage the battery;
- adding many battery-powered accessories to the vehicle while still using the same battery that came with the vehicle;
- long periods of lack of use;
- severe cold; or
- bad habits such as a tendency to leave lights on or the radio running or a door partially open, which automatically switches on interior lights.

As you can see, most of these issues are preventable.

There is a big difference between a battery without enough juice to start the vehicle and one that is permanently dead. Often, with proper care, the former can be recharged and continue operating through the full life of the battery. In fact, one way you can determine whether a vehicle battery is permanently dead is whether it will hold a charge and then recharge through normal vehicle operation. If it won't hold a charge and you find yourself having to jump the battery again and again, it's time to replace the battery.

The symptoms of a failed car battery are that you only hear "clicks" from the ignition when you try to start the vehicle and the lights and radio are very faint, if they operate at all. If the vehicle makes a groaning noise, like the engine is trying its darnedest to start, this may not be a failed battery but some other issue. Also, it's possible that the problems you have are not a failed battery but a problematic alternator. Check the alternator to see if it's loose; if there seems to be some play, determine where and how it is attached and then try to tighten it, usually by tightening one or more screws. Sometimes, tapping once or twice carefully but firmly on the alternator or solenoid will allow a recalcitrant engine to start. The alternator and solenoid are usually found near the front of the vehicle, usually a short distance from the battery; your owner's manual should help you locate them.

You will notice that if there does seem to be some power when you first start, this fades quickly if you have to try repeatedly to turn over the engine.

Once you determine the battery has no—or insufficient—power to start the vehicle, you have two basic choices: try to recharge the battery, usually through jump starting, which can take various forms, or replace the battery, something you don't normally do unless the battery is old (near or past its warranty life span) or won't accept a charge.

Replacement may not be necessary. Even a good or nearly new battery could experience a problem in extreme circumstances like subzero temperatures. A smart rule of thumb is that you should try to recharge the battery and, failing that, replace the battery only if it fails to hold a charge after the recharging or requires frequent recharging.

Before you recharge, there are a couple of things to check. A loose connection or another problem altogether could potentially account for the failure to start the vehicle.

Follow these steps:

1. Open the hood.
2. Inspect the battery for signs of damage.
3. Check that the cables are securely attached to the battery and free of corrosion as shown in figure 7-6.

If the cables are loose on one or both battery posts, tighten them by adjusting the clamps that hold them in place as shown in figure 7-7.

If there is substantial dirt or corrosion on the battery cables and/or posts, you should remove this. A stiff-bristled brush is good for this job, but you should loosen the clamps on each post and remove the battery cables to do this. Once clean, replace the cables and tighten the clamps securely.

Once you have determined the battery is securely connected and, if needed, you have cleaned the battery, posts, and cables and reconnected the battery, try to start the vehicle again. If you

Fig. 7-6: Check that the battery cables are firmly attached and free of corrosion.

Fig. 7-7: The cables should be firmly set on the posts. If not, tighten the clamps that hold the cables in place.

experience the same problem, it's time to try to jump the battery, which you can do a number of different ways, including the following:

- Use jumper cables and a second working vehicle to try to charge the battery on your vehicle enough to let it start.
- Use a jump-start device like one that plugs into household current or into the dashboard lighter.
- If your vehicle has a manual transmission, roll your vehicle or get someone to push it while you try to start it.
- Physically remove the battery and take it to a garage where it can be recharged (the most thorough solution, but it can take some time—up to several hours—and the cost may come close to that of a battery replacement).

Now let's look at the jump-start methods that you can do yourself, some of which require a second working vehicle to accomplish.

Note: A battery that is actually dead will not allow you to jump or recharge it successfully.

Anytime you have reason to suspect you may have trouble with your battery, such as on a frigid morning, keep the lights, radio, and any other accessory device that uses the battery off as you try to start your vehicle. This reduces your chance of draining what little power is present before you succeed in turning over the motor

---

PROCEED WITH CAUTION: THE DANGERS OF JUMP-STARTING

Before you start to jump start a vehicle—whether it's yours or someone else's—you need to appreciate that there is a certain level of danger inherent in the operation. A battery—even dead—packs a certain amount of power. It also contains caustic material, like acid.

While the incidence of injuries from jump-starting a vehicle is statistically low, it is possible for the battery to become damaged during the procedure. In some extreme cases, some batteries have actually exploded. There is also a risk of fire if a spark from the battery ignites gasoline that may be present because of a flooded engine.

Jump Start Using Jumper Cables

Remember that jumper cables were one of the things I recommended you put in your vehicle's emergency kit because they may come in handy for you as well as for helping others caught with a dead battery. But this is one of the solutions that requires another vehicle, one with a fully charged battery, to be successful. So have both jumper cables and another vehicle available before you start. Make certain the jumper cables are clean; if not, wipe them down with a rag.

As noted, you really need to be careful when jumping a battery. The most common error is placing the wrong jumper cable on the wrong post. Be aware that reversing polarity in this way can result in an explosion.

Look at your battery and you should see it is clearly marked, with one terminal designated as positive or "+" and the other labeled as negative or "–" as shown in figure 7-7. If necessary, use a rag to clean the top of both your battery and the one in the "charger" vehicle to be able to see these marks. One big hint: the positive terminal/post is almost always larger than the negative one.

Jumper cables are color coded, usually with a red cable pair and a black cable pair. The red cable pair goes to the positive terminal/post on each vehicle while the black cable pair attaches to the negative terminal/post on each vehicle. Don't confuse them.

The following is one way to jump-start a vehicle, but check your owner's manual before you proceed, and follow the instructions there if they differ from these:

If you have glasses available, especially safety glasses, put these on before you begin to attach the jumper cables.

---

1. Position the second vehicle close to the front of the vehicle to be jumped so that they are close enough for the jumper cables to reach both cars.
2. Shut off the vehicle being used to jump your battery.
3. Open the hoods on both vehicles.
4. Identify the positive and negative terminals/posts on each battery.
5. Take one end of the red jumper cable pair and attach it firmly to the positive terminal on the failed battery as shown in chapter 2 in figure 2-5.
6. Pull the red cable toward the charger vehicle and then attach the other end of the red jumper pair to the positive terminal/post on the battery of the charger vehicle.
7. Take the first of the black jumper cable pair and firmly attach it to the negative terminal/post on the failed battery, then take the other end of the black cable and affix it to the negative terminal/post on the charger vehicle. At this point, you will likely see a spark, which is normal. (Of the manuals I have in front of me, some specify the steps here, while others indicate that the negative cable on the car with the weak battery should be attached to the engine block rather than the negative terminal of the weak battery. Follow your manual's recommendations.)
8. Restart the charger vehicle and rev the engine.
9. After a moment, try to start the vehicle with the failed battery. If it will not start, check the jumper cable placement and adjust as needed before you try again. If necessary, disconnect the jumper cable (note the order in step 11) and clean the terminal/posts on the failed battery.
10. Once the vehicle with the failed battery starts, keep it running for at least 20 to 30 minutes to give the alternator sufficient time to recharge the battery before you turn off the vehicle.
11. Remove the jumper cables in the reverse order in which you first attached them:
12. Remove the black jumper from the negative terminal on the charger vehicle.
13. Remove the black jumper from the negative terminal on the car that wouldn't start before.
14. Take off the red jumper from the positive terminal on the charger vehicle.
15. Detach the red jumper from the positive terminal on the vehicle whose battery needed jumping.
16. Replace the jumper cables in your in-vehicle emergency kit and close the hoods on both vehicles.

Fig. 7-8: The Prestone Portable Power Jump-It shown here is nearly 10 years old, but it has saved the author on a number of extremely cold winter mornings, when even the best car batteries can fail. With the closest car mechanic more than 20 miles away, having such a device is essential.

Using an Electrical Jump-Start Device

Do you live in an area that gets extremely cold in the winter? Or do you happen to be one of those folks who perennially leave the lights on when you park for the night so you frequently come back to a dead battery?

If either of these applies to you, you may want to take a different route than the standard jumper cables jump start, one that doesn't require another vehicle's live battery from which to jump-start your battery.

Several manufacturers like Firestone make a jump-start device like the one shown in figure 7-8, normally priced at between $70 and $100, that will do the job for you. It's reasonably compact in size (smaller than a car battery, anyway), with the cables usually permanently built in. While rather heavy to have to carry any distance, it does have a handle to help you move it between your house or garage and the vehicle.

All you do with these devices is charge them by plugging them into a wall socket. Normally, you let them charge overnight or for at least a few hours. Once the device is charged (and the exact instructions may vary slightly between different models), you simply follow these steps:

1. Take the device out to the vehicle.
2. Attach the appropriate cable to the appropriate battery post as you would for jump-starting, although there is no need for a second vehicle.
3. Let the unit charge the battery for the recommended time, often a minute or two.
4. Try to start the car.

Jump Start from a Lighter Connection

Several manufacturers make a smaller battery-jumping device like the one shown in figure 7-10 that plugs right into the lighter socket located in or near the dashboard. Instead of connecting up cables directly to the battery, you plug one end of the lighter-connected cable into the lighter socket of a running vehicle and the other end into the lighter socket of the vehicle with a weak or dead battery and transfer enough power through it to allow the second vehicle to start.

The process for using such devices is pretty simple:

1. Plug one color-coded end into the lighter socket of a running vehicle with a fully charged battery.
2. Plug the other end into the lighter socket of the vehicle with the problem battery.
3. Let the first vehicle supply power to the second, usually for between five and 10 minutes.
4. Attempt to start the vehicle with the dead battery.

Push Starting a Vehicle with a Dead Battery

The very first thing to consider before you try this method is that pushing or rolling a 2,000-pound—or heavier—vehicle is not a simple or safe operation. Sure, you might get the vehicle to start, but you also may lose control of it or you or those around you may get very seriously injured in the attempt. While you hear this recommended all the time, and almost everyone of a certain age has tried it at one time or another, this is not an operation the author or publisher recommends. No matter how careful you are, you probably won't be able to control all the possible things that can go wrong. Protect yourself and others first, and worry about the vehicle second.

Fig. 7-10: Devices like this one from Wagan Tech plug directly into the lighter socket. Simply remove the lighter itself and set it aside while you connect the 12-volt prong. Check directions to see which color-coded connector goes to which vehicle.

With that said, it is possible that if your vehicle has a manual transmission, you may be able to get the battery to turn over by pushing or rolling the vehicle while you try to turn over the engine. To try this, you probably want to have at least one other person present who can help you move the car. A large vehicle may require several adults to push. Your best bet is to position the vehicle on a small hill or other incline to give you time to roll and start the vehicle.

Before you start, make certain everyone involved knows what to do and takes precautions not to get their feet, hands, or bodies in the way of the wheels or other vehicle parts.

Then:

1. Get behind the wheel inside the car.
2. Turn off any accessories that require the battery such as the lights, radio, heater, and air conditioner.
3. Turn the key in the ignition to the on position but do not try to start the vehicle yet.
4. Depress the clutch pedal.
5. Shift into first gear.
6. Release the hand brake and, once you give the signal to the other person(s) to push, take your foot off the brake pedal.
7. As the vehicle begins to move, release the clutch pedal slowly while also depressing the accelerator pedal and trying to start the vehicle.
8. Once the vehicle is started, keep it running for at least 20 to 30 minutes.

WARNING: While you might be tempted to try to do this all on your own, it's safer with more than one person. For example, if you have to stand partially out of the vehicle to get it to move, you might not be able to hop in the vehicle in time so the car either gets away from you or you get seriously injured.

The older the battery, or the more extensive its history of requiring jump starts, the more likely it is that you should replace it as soon as possible.

Maintaining Good Battery Health

Even though the time required and the likelihood of disasters in jump starting aren't that significant, this is not something you want to do frequently.

The best way to avoid this is to properly maintain the battery—and the rest of the vehicle. Measures you can take include the following:

WHAT TO DO ONCE THE VEHICLE STARTS

Once you manage to jump start your battery and turn over the engine, don't assume you're back to normal. You aren't, at least not yet. Very likely, you have just supplied enough juice to let the battery work to start the vehicle; it may deplete again very quickly.

The normal operation of the vehicle can serve to recharge the battery. Yet this usually only occurs if you drive for a period of time after jump-starting. A short trip to a store, for example, may find you with the battery dead again once you hop back in for the return trip. A 15- or 20-minute commute, however, is more likely to leave the battery with enough power to let you start it again in an hour or even at the end of your workday.

- Being certain you turn off the radio/CD player, lights, windshield wipers, and any other accessory run from the battery when you turn off the vehicle
- Following manufacturer recommendations for adding water, if required, to the cells in the battery
- Keeping the battery terminals clear of corrosion and dirt (chapter 5 tells you how to do this using a stiff brush) and removing excess dirt from the battery itself
- Checking the tautness of your fan belt, since a loose fan belt may interfere with the battery's ability to recharge properly or maintain its charge
- Securing the battery firmly in its mount near the engine; a battery that isn't secured may move about and work the cables loose and/or damage the battery or other parts of the vehicle
- Replacing a problematic alternator or solenoid promptly

WARNING: Because of the substances like acid found in vehicle batteries, it's important that you dispose of them properly. Old batteries should not sit for a prolonged period in your garage or in the yard since they may become damaged and leak. Most communities today offer some type of recycling program to allow you to turn in old batteries—check to see what your municipality or state provides in that regard. Also, many auto parts stores and garages will accept used batteries. You may be subject to a small fee per battery— often between $1 and $5—as a handling charge for disposal.

Considerations in Replacing an Auto Battery

Different vehicles require different batteries. Variations in battery types include how they mount inside the vehicle, whether they require regular or no maintenance, and their overall capability to handle power demands of accessory items within the vehicle (for example, power windows, doors, and door locks, electronically adjusted seats, and special heating and cooling options like seat warmers).

Consult your owner's manual for battery replacement recommendations. Your garage or auto parts store should be able to match you up with a suitable replacement, even if you opt not to pay for the exact model specified by the owner's manual.

Note the word "suitable." Buying either a less or more powerful battery than the one originally provided with the vehicle is usually not a smart thing to do. An underpowered battery will be subject to a shortened life span and may require more effort on your part; an overpowered battery at best probably won't do anything for you but will cost more to purchase.

Once you have your replacement battery, follow these steps to install it:

1. Open the hood.
2. Use a screwdriver or other tool to release the clamps holding the current battery in place.
3. Remove the cables from the battery.
4. Lift the old battery out and set it aside.
5. Clean the cables and connections of the battery using a clean rag and a stiff-bristled brush.
6. Use a small broom or rag to clean out the tray or area where the battery sits.
7. Remove any advertising or attachments from the replacement battery.
8. Lift the new battery up and install it into the area vacated by the previous battery.
9. Reconnect the cables and tighten the clamps, being sure that the front of the battery is positioned toward the front of the car so you aren't reversing polarity.
10. Close the hood.
11. Dispose of the old battery properly (see sidebar).
12. Start the vehicle to be sure the new battery works properly. If the vehicle will not start, check your battery connections and be sure you removed any corrosion, then try again.

Help! My Battery Light Comes On and Stays Lit!

What should you do if this happens to you?

First, besides following the standard advice of not panicking, check your owner's manual to see what it may state about your battery light.

Next, understand that the battery light on most vehicles does not actually correspond to the battery itself. It normally won't light if the battery is low on power or otherwise in trouble. Instead, it lights if the alternator is not working properly to charge and recharge the battery, so the problem is likely with your alternator.

If you're driving when you see the light engage, you probably don't need to pull over—at least not immediately. You still should have some time in which you can use the car before you need to stop—or a dead battery stops you. But you should:

- turn off any unnecessary accessories that require the battery like the radio, heater/cooler and any nonrequired lights;
- try not to make any additional demands on the battery;
- avoid a situation where you must turn off the engine, since you may not be able to start it again; and
- if at all possible, drive to an auto parts shop or a garage; if you can, leave the vehicle running while you go inside.

A garage—or even a well-equipped and customer-oriented auto parts store—should be able to perform an alternator test to determine whether this component is failing and needs replacement. It's also possible that another issue, such as a loose fan belt or even a loose alternator itself—is the cause of the problem. On some vehicles, you can see the battery light appear if the battery is low on water, a detail that should be checked as part of regular battery maintenance when doing other maintenance on your vehicle.

If you can't get to a garage or service professional immediately, try to take these steps until you can:

1. Try to get home or somewhere else that will be convenient should the vehicle not start again. Here, a charged cell phone comes in handy in case you need to call for a ride.
2. Pull over and turn off the vehicle. If it's dark, you may need a flashlight to help you check under the hood.
3. Release the hood and open it.
4. As soon as the engine compartment is cool enough to let you touch what's inside, check to be sure the battery cables are firmly attached and free of corrosion. If they are loose, try to tighten them. Also be sure that the battery is firmly seated in its compartment and can't be easily moved—an unsecured battery may rock back and forth, causing a problem (see figure 7-11).
5. Try to locate your alternator. Using a flashlight as needed, locate and make certain the alternator and fan belt are attached and undamaged and that no connections to the alternator appear loose.

Fig. 7-11: A loose battery can make it difficult for the alternator to work with it; over time, the battery may become damaged. If the housing or tray that holds the battery in place is damaged, visit your local auto parts store and see what they might have to help you resecure the battery.

6. If you have a battery that requires maintenance, follow instructions with the battery to open the cells at the top of the battery to check the water level. You may need to add water—and distilled water may be required—if the level is low.

7. Try to restart the vehicle and see whether the battery light is now out. If the light is still on, make arrangements to take it to the garage as soon as possible.

TIGHTENING A LOOSE FAN BELT OR REPLACING A BROKEN ONE

The fan belt is usually located at the very front of the engine compartment, often between the radiator and the engine block, as shown in figure 7-12. With the vehicle turned off and cool, place your hand on the fan belt and determine if there is any slack. Normally, the belt will feel quite taut, yet you still should be able to push it and notice between one-half and three-quarters of an inch in slack. Anything tighter than that is too tight and could damage the fan belt and even the engine. Anything much looser than that means the fan belt will not serve its purpose.

When a fan belt begins to fail—which it does by tearing or breaking—you're apt to know it. You might be driving along and notice the vehicle seems to be losing power. It's possible you may notice that the lights begin to dim or the radio does not function. You also may experience a certain roughness in the way the vehicle handles and a sense that you're really having to push the vehicle by flooring the accelerator just to move along at 30 to 40 miles per hour. Also, the engine temperature may rise, perhaps to a state where it overheats. If your dashboard has an alternator light, you may see this come on.

In fact, the minute you stop driving, even if you just brake rather than turn off the ignition, the

Fig. 7-12: The fan belt is usually readily identifiable because it is located in a triangular configuration near the very front of the vehicle.

vehicle is apt to die altogether. Naturally, it will pick the worst possible place like the middle of a busy intersection or perhaps somewhere out in the middle of nowhere.

The worst part is that it will likely be impossible to restart the vehicle without replacing the fan belt. Once a loose or loosening fan belt reaches the stage where you have this kind of situation, you probably won't be able to tighten it as a short-term solution. Yet it's worth checking, so let's cover that first.

If the vehicle has just been operated, you should let it cool for at least a half hour; opening the hood may hasten cooling, at least with some vehicles and designs. Then follow the instructions under Tightening a Loose Fan Belt.

Tightening a Loose Fan Belt

First, appreciate that while the fan belt should be reasonably taut, it should not be so tight that it may break as it moves. A tiny amount of slack—up to about a half-inch on most vehicles—is acceptable. Anything more than that needs adjustment.

Next, check your owner's manual for any special instructions about your fan belt. Many fan belts can be adjusted just fine without special tools, but some—along with other belts in the

Savvy Tip

A squeal coming from the engine when the vehicle is being operated is often a good indicator of a loose or badly worn fan belt. Rather than wait for the fan belt to fail once you hear the squeal, inspect the fan belt and tighten it if it is loose or replace it if it is worn.

Fig. 7-13: Locate the nut at the front of the fan belt assembly. This must be loosened and removed to check, clean, and replace the belt. A 22mm or 7/8″ socket wrench is often the best tool for removing the nut at the front of the fan belt assembly. Remember to put the nut where you can easily find it later.

vehicle—are designed in such a way that they can really only be adjusted or replaced by professionals with proper tools.

For this procedure, you'll need a wrench large enough to remove a large-size nut and a screwdriver that can be used temporarily to secure the fan belt while you remove the nut to adjust the belt. A cloth suitable for removing loose grit is a good idea as well.

A large nut located at the front of the fan belt assembly (see figure 7-13) usually holds everything secure, starting with the adjusting bolt on which this nut is mounted. You may need to use a rag to clean this area in order to see what is what. This nut usually must be loosened and then removed to tighten the fan belt itself. The belt, you will notice, is often positioned between pulleys in a triangular configuration.

Shims—small black rings located along the belt assembly—allow you to adjust the belt's tension. Adding shims increases the slack while removing shims tightens the belt. Extra shims are often found stored somewhere near the fan belt assembly. If you need to replace your fan belt, you may also want to replace the shims, taking care that you get the right kind for your vehicle. Even if you only need to tighten the belt, you should replace existing shims if any are damaged. The same is true for the pulleys through which the belt is threaded.

Follow these steps:

1. Locate a wrench suitable to work with the size nut available on the fan belt assembly.
2. Determine how best to hold the belt steady while you remove the nut. Sometimes a carefully placed screwdriver inserted between the holes of the pulley and not against the fan belt itself—but without damaging the belt—will work.
3. With the fan belt held in place, remove the nut (refer to figure 7-13) and set it aside.

4. Use the cloth to remove loose grit and debris from the belt and belt assembly.

5. Inspect the belt for signs of wear, using other parts of the belt for comparison. Place your hand in a free, unobstructed area and move the belt through your fingers (see figure 7-14). Look for cracks, breaks, or irregularities of any kind. If all appears fine, proceed to step 6. But if you notice wear, replace the belt as soon as possible.

6. To tighten the fan belt, note the location of the shims—there are often five along each length of the triangle between pulleys—and then determine how best to remove a single shim, checking tautness after the removal. (You do not want to remove all the shims.) Often, a shim can be removed if you cut it away using heavy-duty scissors or some other snipping device. All remaining shims should be equally distanced from one another along the length of the belt. (One of the ways fan belts fail is that they become dry from all the heating and begin to crack. If you find an irregularity during your inspection, you should replace the fan belt as soon as possible.)

7. Replace the nut on the adjusting bolt and tighten it.

8. Start the car, let it run a moment, and then turn it off again. This step is necessary to see how the belt performs once it's been put to work.

9. Recheck the belt's tightness. If it appears properly tight—with just a one-half- to three-quarter-inch slack, you're done. If not, you may need to repeat the previous steps to remove an additional shim.

Replacing the Fan Belt

It's very important that you get the exact type of fan belt you need for your make and model of vehicle. Fan belts are usually only available through a garage or auto parts store.

Some fan belt replacement kits include a special tool to help you perform the replacement. It may be worth any small price difference to buy a kit that includes the tool rather than just the belt itself (the belts themselves are reasonably inexpensive considering how long they last and how much abuse they take).

Once you have the replacement fan belt:

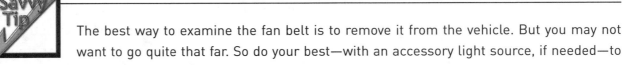

The best way to examine the fan belt is to remove it from the vehicle. But you may not want to go quite that far. So do your best—with an accessory light source, if needed—to inspect the belt for signs of damage with the belt still in place.

1. Remove the nut at the end of the adjusting bolt on the fan belt assembly.

2. Either use the special tool in the replacement kit to hold each pulley in place while you remove the belt or use a screwdriver inserted in the holes of the pulley, which also serves to stop the fan blades from turning.

3. Once the old belt is off, follow directions on the replacement package—or in your owner's manual—to replace the belt. This usually involves placing five fresh shims on the shaft between the two main halves of the pulley mechanism. Then seat the belt as directed and tighten it. Constantly recheck belt tension as you work. Remember, you want one-half to three-quarters of an inch of slack. More slack is too loose; less slack is too tight (see figure 7-13).

4. When the belt seems properly seated and secure, tighten the nut over the adjusting bolt again and turn the engine over briefly, then turn it off again.

5. Check the tightness of the belt after the engine turnover and adjust belt tension as needed. You may need to remove one of the shims you have installed, but normally, you should place all shims into the assembly until you determine whether one must be removed to cure slackness.

6. Retest by turning the engine over again and then shutting it off. Then check once more until you are satisfied the belt is snug without being overly tight.

WARNING: If you are not convinced you have installed the belt correctly or notice problems after replacement, have this checked by a professional. Prolonged vehicle operation without the fan belt properly secured can damage the belt, the assembly, and/or the engine.

Preventing Problems

Your absolute best bet to prevent a situation where your fan belt fails is to regularly check it as part of your routine automotive maintenance. It's probably fair to say that most fan belts fail prematurely simply because no one noticed they were becoming loose. Once you notice signs of wear or cracking or other damage, plan to replace the fan belt as soon as possible.

Now that you've successfully handled five of the most common problems you may experience with your vehicle, it's time to move up to handle five more, including coping with the very worst of all: the engine that just won't start. Turn to chapter 8 and learn what to do.

8 COPING WITH THE TOP 10 COMMON PROBLEMS, PART 2

◆ Stop blowing hot and cold

◆ Quieting a noisy muffler

◆ Doctoring a car that won't start

◆ Curing a car running rough

◆ Overcoming poor fuel/oil consumption

You're about to take a big step by working with problems that can be harder to troubleshoot and solve. Here, you will tackle issues like a vehicle that runs roughly or won't start at all and a vehicle that is suddenly consuming more gas or oil than normal.

These may be problems you have traditionally depended on a mechanic or garage to solve, but you may be surprised about how much of this leg work and analysis you can do yourself before you shell out the money for professional assistance.

Of course there is no guarantee you will be able to fix these problems all on your own. You may still need to call on experts. But you're going to grow your knowledge of your vehicle by trying to find your own solutions. No longer will you have to confront a vehicle that won't start without having the foggiest idea of what to do.

Hopefully, as part of this, you will save some money, because if eventually you do need to take your vehicle to the pros, you can tell them what you've figured out and what you have already tried yourself. The mechanic may be able to do a better job for you if you can demonstrate some knowledge of the basics and give him or her smart pointers about the situation at hand.

So without further ado, let's roll up our sleeves and get to work!

Overcoming Heating and/or Cooling Problems and an Overheating Engine

While it might seem that there are few things worse than having to take a long drive during which you can't get the heating or cooling system to keep the passenger compartment comfortable, there is something much worse. An engine that overheats even once can do damage to one or more components under the hood. The more frequently the overheating occurs, the more extensive the damage can be. You can literally cook the engine to the point where it needs to be overhauled or even replaced.

In this section, you will explore the kinds of issues that can contribute to your inability to heat or cool the passenger compartment as well as correct problems that can lead to engine overheating. Many of these difficulties are ones you can handle yourself, without extensive knowledge or fancy, expensive equipment.

But before you start, here's a word of warning. If you make your best attempts to fix the situation yourself and still notice that your temperature gauge creeps ever upwards as you drive or idle in traffic, seek out a good professional. You can't afford to ignore the situation; doing so will leave you without your vehicle.

Is Your Vehicle Overheating?

The heating/cooling system strives to strike a proper balance between keeping the engine from getting too hot and the passengers from getting too cold.

Some of the common causes of engine overheating include the following:

- Running the air conditioning on high for prolonged periods of time
- Generally poor maintenance
- An engine in dire need of servicing and repair
- A corrupted fluid mix of antifreeze and water in the radiator or running with too low a fluid level in the radiator
- A malfunctioning thermostat

- Operating the vehicle with a low oil level
- Long intervals between oil changes; once the oil begins to break down, it no longer provides the same level of lubrication and protection for moving parts of the engine
- A defective water pump
- A damaged radiator or radiator hose
- A loose or damaged fan belt

Maintenance obviously plays a major role here. If you regularly check your hoses as shown in figure 8-1, look for leaks such as from the radiator or its hose(s). Checking hoses and watching the fluid levels in your radiator and adding more water and antifreeze as needed (remember, you usually need a 50-50 mix) will usually enable you to catch some or most of the problems that can contribute to engine overheating before the temperature gauge actually starts registering in the red. Thus, if you are not doing regular maintenance, reconsider.

Now let's look at what you need to check to resolve the problem. First, it's not terribly unusual to have a vehicle overheat on a really hot day sitting in gridlocked traffic. If the overheating happens once and there seems to be a good cause for it, just perform your standard maintenance and watch to be sure it does not recur.

Once you notice, however, that the engine is frequently overheating, you need to take steps to identify the source of the problem and correct it. You may actually discover more than one thing you need to correct: a damaged hose and a low radiator fluid level, for example. For this reason, you need to do some systematic troubleshooting.

Cooling an Overheating Engine

The very first thing you need to do is get the engine temperature back in normal operating range to prevent any (further) damage. One thing you cannot do is continue to operate the

Fig. 8-1: Periodically check your hoses, like the radiator hoses shown here, to be sure they are free of cracks or damage that may result in a leak.

Fig. 8-2: Make it a point to consult the temperature gauge on your dashboard regularly as you drive. When the engine has been running for a while, the needle should be at or near the midway mark. If you notice a tendency for the gauge to register very low (except when the car is cold) or very high, you need to take time to investigate.

vehicle for a prolonged period of time with the temperature gauge (see figure 8-2) showing in the red range.

One way to cool the engine down is to pull the vehicle over and pop the hood. It may take an hour or more to sufficiently lower the temperature, and there is no sure bet that the engine won't begin to overheat as soon as you're back on the road. So let's look at some of the other, more effective measures you can take.

If the overheating occurs while you're stuck in traffic, turn off anything that may be making heating demands, such as the air conditioner, if you have one. If you are sitting there with no chance of moving for several minutes, turn the engine off until you can move again. Also—and this may be uncomfortable on a hot day—turn on your heater; this will direct hot air away from the engine to blow into the passenger compartment, which, alone, may be enough to drop the overall temperature.

Then, as soon as you can, pull the vehicle over into a safe spot where you can spend several minutes checking it over without fear of being struck by other traffic. Also, turn on your hazard lights. It helps if you have a gallon of water on hand, in case you need to add additional fluid to the cooling system. You may want to try to keep a gallon of water in the vehicle, especially during the hot summer months, for this purpose. The water does not have to be—in fact, it should not be—ice cold. Adding very cold water to a very hot engine can crack the radiator.

Next:

1. Turn off the engine.
2. Open the hood.

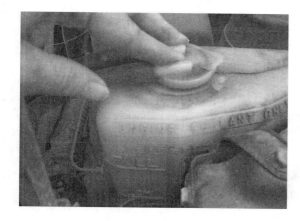

Fig. 8-3: The radiator should have at least two hoses: one that mounts near the top and another that attaches near the bottom of the radiator. These hoses have clamps at either end that should be closed. Replace a missing or broken clamp immediately.

3. Let the vehicle sit for at least several minutes to cool a bit before you try to do anything.

4. Inspect the radiator and its hoses for any signs of damage or looseness, as shown in figure 8-3.

5. If you have some newspaper available, place some beneath the radiator on the ground below the front of the vehicle to see if there is evidence of a radiator leak. A few drips may mean nothing, but if the paper becomes saturated, you may have a radiator or radiator hose leak.

6. If you notice a loose clamp or tear in a hose, either secure the clamp or use heat-resistant tape to try to seal the hose again. If the radiator itself appears damaged, you probably need to call a tow truck immediately; the vehicle should not be driven in this condition.

7. Consult your owner's manual to see if it offers any specific directions for dealing with an overheating engine or checking radiator fluid levels. On some vehicles, the radiator overflow reservoir as well as the radiator itself is pressurized so you may need to wait until the car cools adequately before you try (carefully) to remove the top and add fluid if needed.

Savvy Tip

Whenever you're dealing with an overheating engine or other cooling or heating problems, consider rolling a complete radiator flush (documented in chapter 5) and an oil change (covered in chapter 4) into your routine. Degraded coolant and dirty oil can both contribute to overheating.

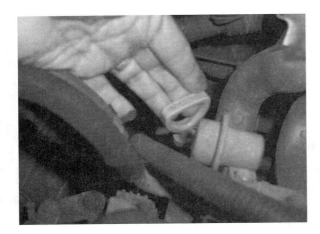

Fig. 8-4: Check your oil level at least once a week. Have spare oil available—the correct grade for your vehicle—to add as needed.

8. Check the fluid level in your radiator overflow reservoir as shown in figure 8-4. If it's low, adding at least water (coolant, too, if you have it available) to the reservoir is a good idea.

9. Check your oil level. If it's low, add more oil as soon as possible (assuming you don't carry a spare container of oil in your trunk).

Checking for a Stuck Thermostat

The thermostat in your vehicle has a vital job: to control how the coolant mix is distributed based on whether the engine is cold, warm, or too hot. When the engine is cold, such as when you first start it in the morning, the thermostat tells the system not to send out coolant because there is no need. Then, as the engine begins to warm, the thermostat gives the go-ahead for the flow of coolant, increasing the amount as the demands require.

A stuck thermostat—which can come about through the accumulation of dirt and debris, the age of the device, or some failure of the device itself—means it is no longer doing its job as coolant controller. Thus, it's not going to adjust the coolant level as the engine heats up and the temperature will rise quickly because there is an insufficient amount of water and antifreeze.

On many vehicles, the thermostat is a rather low-cost part (frequently priced at under $20), so many people choose to replace this whenever they see the temperature on the vehicle rise and they've determined the radiator is functioning correctly and has the right fluid level. But you may not want to do that unless your vehicle is several years old. Not every thermostat is inexpensive, either.

Fig. 8-5: The top radiator hose is often about 2 inches in diameter, black, with clamps at either end.

There's a relatively simple, low-tech test you can try to determine if the thermostat is operating properly. It's not foolproof, but it's a pretty adequate indicator.

Follow these steps:

1. Start the engine and allow it to get warm (don't let it overheat, however).
2. Once the engine is warm, shut it off.
3. Open the hood.
4. Locate the topmost radiator hose (see figure 8-5). This is typically black and made of rubber or a very similar material. This connects to the top side of the radiator, usually with metal clamps at either end.
5. Feel the upper hose to tell how warm it is. Don't be shy, although you don't want to burn your fingers or hand.
6. Now find the lower radiator hose that connects to the bottom of the radiator.
7. Feel the lower hose to determine its temperature.
8. Compare the temperature difference between the two hoses. If one hose is almost cool while the other is much, much warmer, this could signify a thermostat that is stuck in the closed position. If so, replace the thermostat. Keep in mind that in normal operation, the top radiator hose usually does not get quite as hot as the lower hose.

Here's another way to test a thermostat:

1. Open the hood and remove the radiator cap as shown in figure 8-6. Use extreme caution! Set the cap aside for the time being.
2. Start the engine. Make certain the hand brake is engaged.
3. Go back to the front of the car. Don't position yourself at the front of a car that is

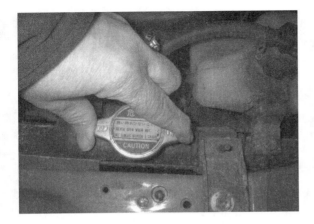

Fig. 8-6: Remove the radiator cap before the engine begins to heat. If the engine is already warm, let it cool for a bit. Use extreme caution as you slowly remove the radiator cap. Fluid can spray up and the pressure can be so high that the cap is blown from your grip.

Fig. 8-7: Check the level in the radiator coolant tank, as shown here. If you must do this in the dark, you may want to press a flashlight into service to monitor the fluid level inside the radiator.

     pointed downhill unless you really trust your hand brake. Place a cement block or other heavy implement in front of your rear tire to make sure the vehicle does not roll.

4. Look at the level of coolant-water mixture in the radiator while the engine warms (see figure 8-7). You should notice the level begin to drop as the temperature comes up because coolant flows out to cool the engine. If there is no appreciable drop in radiator fluid level, you may very well have a thermostat that is stuck in the closed position.

There is a third thermostat test, but this one is a little trickier and more time consuming and carries a risk of getting burned. For this, you need to physically remove the thermostat from the vehicle (learn how to do that in the section "Replacing Your Thermostat"). Place the device in a pan or cup of hot (up to 200 degrees Fahrenheit) water. As the part warms, you should see its aperture begin to open. If the aperture does not open or opens only slightly, the thermostat is stuck and needs replacement.

Thermostats Can Stick Open, Too

While a thermostat that is stuck closed is usually what creates the most problems in overheating and damage to an engine, you can also have a thermostat stuck open. When this happens, the engine never reaches normal operating temperature because the coolant-water mix is flowing too freely.

If you notice your dashboard temperature gauge never quite hits the normal level anymore (and as a vehicle gets older, the tendency is for an engine to increase rather than decrease in temperature), you may have a stuck thermostat. Replacement of the thermostat is needed.

A stuck thermostat should also be suspected when the vents in your car only seem to blow cold or hot air.

About Choosing a Replacement Thermostat

Besides picking a thermostat designed to work with your make and model of vehicle, there are a couple of other things you should know about the replacement process. For example, many thermostats have a rating level of 160, 180, or 195 degrees Fahrenheit. You should select a thermostat of the same temperature type as the one you are replacing; your owner's manual may tell you what to buy.

There are two major types of thermostats: standard and dual-acting. The latter has a special component that acts to shut down the bypass circuit. Again, the replacement you buy should match the type you currently have.

Good auto parts stores stock a wide range of vehicle thermostats. If you have an unusual make or model that requires a special order, the store can usually get it for you within 24 to 48 hours. When you go in, be sure to ask if a gasket comes with the thermostat, since many vehicles require you to replace the gasket that goes with the thermostat at the same time.

WARNING: If you replace a normal thermostat with a dual-acting one in some vehicles, you can create a situation where the new thermostat acts like it is stuck open. If you notice these symptoms after replacing your thermostat, check the packaging to see if you mistakenly added a dual-acting thermostat.

Replacing Your Thermostat

With some exceptions, it doesn't take an electrical engineer or a master mechanic to remove and replace a problem thermostat. On some vehicles, the job is pretty easy and fast, too.

The thermostat is located in its own housing, usually positioned near the front of the engine close to the top-mounted radiator hose. The thermostat must be removed from its housing along with its gasket, if present, if the gasket is in a deteriorated or damaged condition.

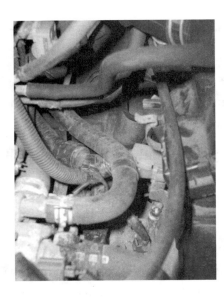

Fig. 8-8: Disconnect the topmost radiator hose on the end that connects with the thermostat housing.

Before you start, have a screwdriver handy, along with fresh water and coolant. A rag to clean the thermostat housing is a also a good idea.

Then complete these steps:

1. Open the hood.
2. Locate the thermostat housing. Your owner's manual may or may not indicate where it is, but accessory manuals like Chilton's almost always will. If you can't find it and your reference materials don't include it in diagrams, look between the engine block itself and the top-mounted radiator hose.
3. Once you find the housing, disconnect the top radiator hose (you usually need to remove one end of its clamp) as shown in figure 8-8.
4. Pull the housing out gently. If there is a cover in place, remove the cover and set it aside.
5. Before you take out the thermostat, note how it is installed. You want to mount the new one just like the old one.
6. Remove the thermostat itself along with any decaying bits of gasket, if present. Set the thermostat aside and use a rag to clean up the interior of the housing. Check any remaining gasket material and determine whether you need a replacement gasket (this should come automatically with the replacement, but check when you buy the thermostat).
7. Insert the new thermostat and, if needed, the fresh gasket. With most thermostats, the top of the device will face toward the engine block. If the thermostat has a bell-like

Savvy Tip

A thermostat is usually expected to last between two and three years, although some last much, much longer and others may fail within the first year. Once you encounter a problem with overheating or cold air blowing from the vents, check the thermostat and replace it if necessary.

valve on one side, this valve—called a jiggle valve—needs to be on top to allow bubbles to pass through.

8. If there is a cover to the housing, put this on.

9. Place the housing back in its original position and bolt or clamp it down (depending on how it was secured before).

10. Reconnect the topmost radiator hose.

11. Next, check the fluid level in the radiator and radiator overflow reservoir. Be prepared to add a mix of water and coolant, as needed. Leave the radiator cap off for the time being.

12. Start the engine.

13. Return to the front of the car to monitor the fluid level. If needed, add more, but leave some room in the neck of the radiator to allow air to rise to the surface and escape. As the engine warms, the level should drop. If the level seems to get very low, you will probably want to add more coolant-water mix once you turn off the engine.

14. Go inside the vehicle and turn on the heater full-blast.

15. Recheck the fluid level in the radiator.

16. If everything seems fine, once the engine reaches normal operating temperature, turn the heater off and then shut down the engine.

17. Check the fluid level once more. Add more as needed.

18. Replace the radiator cap, close the hood, and clean up.

19. If you are keeping notes either in a vehicle journal or directly inside your owner's manual, jot down the date and what you did, along with the replacement thermostat information.

WARNING: For the first several days after you install the replacement thermostat, keep an eye on the engine temperature gauge. If you notice any problems, make certain you installed the new thermostat correctly. If you continue to experience overheating and/or cooling trouble, investigate what else may be wrong.

Keeping Warm While You Drive

Various problems can contribute to the inability to get the passenger compartment warm enough. These issues include the following:

- A faulty vehicle heater or heater core that needs to be inspected and repaired by a professional
- A malfunctioning fan that doesn't circulate warm air efficiently
- A hole, leak, or break in the heater line that prevents warm air from reaching the cabin
- A thermostat stuck open, causing so much coolant to circulate in the engine that there isn't hot enough air to transfer into the passenger compartment, a condition that can also be caused by the wrong type of thermostat having been installed
- Something obstructing the push of warm air up into the cabin

The first three issues listed really call for a professional, while thermostat problems were addressed earlier in this chapter. So let's look at the obstruction issue.

Ever turn on the fan in your vehicle and get blinded by dust, bits of dried leaves, and other debris? Often, such material works its way down from the windshield well—where the wipers are located—and gets into the system that supplies air to the passenger compartment. Depending on the design of the vehicle, this debris can actually block the passage of warm air into the cabin.

You can avoid this problem by regularly brushing material out of the windshield well of your vehicle. Avoid turning on the fan when you haven't taken the time to clean out the debris first.

You can also try opening all the vents into the vehicle (as illustrated in figure 8-9) and then turning the fan on full blast to try to flush any material out of the system. Plan to vacuum out the vehicle after you do this, because you're apt to bring into the passenger compartment mold spores, leaf fragments, pollen—all manner of debris that rains down on your windshield in the process of driving or leaving your vehicle parked.

Air Conditioning Usually Requires Professional Service

If your vehicle has air conditioning, try to find out when it was last serviced. This is the kind of entry that should be noted in your owner's manual or your vehicle journal.

If it's been more than a year or two, make an appointment to take the vehicle in. While your owner's manual may point out filters or other parts that you can easily replace yourself, air conditioning itself often calls for professional servicing by folks who can dispose of any drained fluids properly.

Fig. 8-9: Open your vents before you turn the fan on full blast to try to loosen and blow out anything that may be in the air line.

Dealing with a Noisy Muffler

A loud muffler certainly doesn't need a lot of fancy diagnosis. You can hear the problem and you may see it, too, in the form of a loose exhaust or tailpipe or one that is dragging on the ground.

Yet noise really isn't your biggest problem, nor is the ticket from the highway patrol you may receive. Once the exhaust system begins to lose integrity, as it does when a hole is punched in the muffler by a rock or the edges of a pothole or the tailpipe works loose, deadly but odorless fumes can enter your passenger compartment, some of the worst of which can sicken or even kill you. In addition, a dragging tailpipe or muffler produces sparks as it hits the pavement, which for a gasoline-fueled vehicle can be a recipe for disaster.

This is a case where the sooner you take action, the better. For example, buying and installing an inexpensive auto clamp to secure a loose tailpipe like that shown in figure 8-10 can prevent any more damage from being done to the exhaust system; this could buy you a year or more before you need to replace the muffler, provided the rest of the system is intact and working well.

But even if the tailpipe is actually broken and/or detached, there are still a few things you can do to limp along until you can get to the garage or muffler shop. Let's briefly cover each, with the understanding that both require the vehicle to be cool enough so you can touch the tailpipe, which can become extremely hot since it's venting fumes from the engine.

Here's method one:

1. If some part of the tailpipe is about to fall off and you don't think it can be saved, even

Fig. 8-10: Once you get the right clamp, find the best place to secure the loose tailpipe to the underside.

in the short term, use a rag to wrap the pipe and twist the broken part free. If most of the tailpipe is destroyed, however, you need to get it to the shop immediately.

2. Locate either a wire coat hanger or some mechanic's wire (available at many hardware stores as well as auto parts stores). Cut and bend the coat hanger or cut off a decent length of the mechanic's wire.

3. Wrap the wire around the tailpipe and then wrap it around some sturdy fixture on the underside of the vehicle to try to secure the pipe until you can get to the garage or muffler shop.

4. You may want to drive a short distance and then check the wire to see if it's staying in place. Readjust it as needed.

Here's method two:

1. With the tailpipe clear, use something to measure the diameter of the pipe to get at least a rough idea of the size.

2. Try to locate a tin can that is just slightly larger than the diameter of the pipe. Open both ends of the can.

3. Slide the can over the broken or rusted-through part of the tail pipe to make sure it fits in place. If all you can find is a larger can but you have tin snips or some other cutting device, you can cut the can along the seams and then wrap it around the tailpipe. Exercise care that you do not cut yourself.

4. Install two nut clamps to either side of the tin can to hold it in place.

5. Check your work after it is installed.

A LOW-TECH HEATING SOLUTION

Do you have a vehicle like an older SUV that simply won't heat the passenger cabin as thoroughly as it once did?

Once you explore and try to fix other things that may be wrong, like a damaged or dirty thermostat or defective hoses, here's an idea that has worked for me and others on a number of vehicles to provide heat in the dead of winter.

Cut a piece of thick cardboard roughly the size of the front grille of the vehicle and insert it in the grille. This will block some of the coldest air from entering the vhicle and reduce the amount of heat that escapes. The result should be a warmer passenger compartment.

Don't forget to make an appointment at the garage or muffler shop. These techniques should not be used for more than a few days at most.

DOCTORING A VEHICLE THAT JUST WON'T START

Some mornings, nothing seems to go right. It's almost a relief when you slip behind the wheel of your car and put the key in the ignition. At least until you turn the key and nothing happens. Or all you hear is a "rrr-rrr-rrr."

Don't panic, at least not yet. You can troubleshoot this by checking a few things before you call for a tow truck that may not come for an hour or two anyway.

WARNING: Avoid holding the ignition key in the Start—as opposed to the On—position for longer than 10 seconds. Doing so can actually damage the starter or the ignition mechanism and can require a very costly repair.

Where a Diagnostic Trouble Code Reader Comes in Handy

If you happened to purchase one of the diagnostic trouble code readers first discussed back in chapter 1, you may want to put it into service for situations like this. Doing so may be able to cut your troubleshooting time down to a fraction of what it may be otherwise.

Visit BAT Auto Technical's TroubleCodes.net at www.troublecodes.net/technical/ (see figure 8-11) and you can tie into a resource that lists and explains trouble codes sorted by many different makes, even Yugos and Daihatsus.

Troubleshooting Steps

First, determine exactly what behavior is being displayed. This is where you play detective.

For example:

- If you just hear clicks or absolutely nothing, it's possible your battery is dead. Chapter 7 details several different ways you can jump start the battery. If you notice a light switch that has been left on or a door not fully closed, a dead battery is a very strong possibility. If your lights or radio work, however, a dead battery is not the culprit.
- If the vehicle tries to start but the engine is simply not turning over with enough power to engage, this may indicate a drained battery or loose battery connections, a problem with the starter or alternator (this probably will require a mechanic), or low or corrupted oil (check the oil level and plan to do an oil change ASAP).
- If the vehicle tries to start but the engine never fires, something could be up with the plugs or points. A spark plug could be dirty (and removing it and cleaning it may help). If there has just been rain or the vehicle has conked out while driving through a large puddle, you may need to use something like starter spray or WD-40 to try to dry the points enough to run.
- If the engine turns over but keeps dying, you have a different problem. Likely, this is the result of really poor vehicle maintenance. A tune-up and oil change may help, but if it does not, you may need to have the vehicle diagnosed by a professional mechanic.

As you're doing your analysis, don't forget to check the dashboard warning lights. Are any lit?

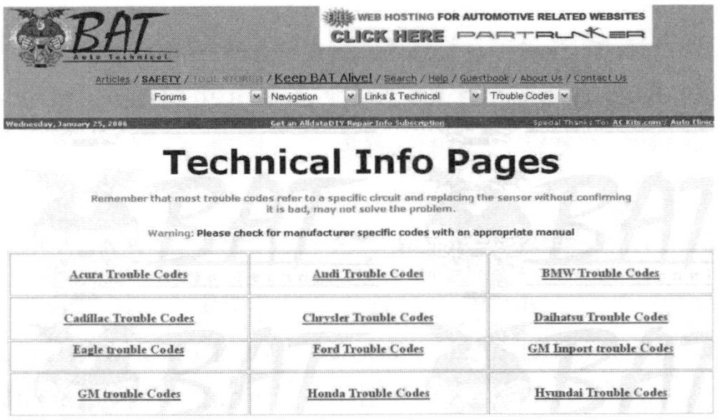

Fig. 8-11: This free Web site (www.troublecodes.net/technical) lists and explains many of the trouble codes your vehicle's onboard computer may generate.

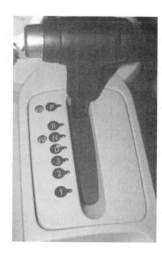

Fig. 8-12: Always check your gear setting before you try to start your vehicle.

This can give you a big hint as to what may be wrong. See the section "About Your Dashboard Warning Lights" in this chapter.

Also try these diagnostic steps:

- If your lights or radio won't come on, check the battery connections beneath the hood. Remove any corrosion from the cables and posts. If necessary, jump start.
- Note what gear you are trying to start from as shown in figure 8-12; most vehicles need to be in Park or Neutral to allow you to start the vehicle.
- Look beneath the hood for any other loose cables and connections (see figure 8-13). If you took the time, as suggested earlier in the book, to familiarize yourself with how components and hoses are connected when the vehicle is working well, it should be easier to spot a problem.
- While under the hood, check the fan belt (discussed in detail in chapter 7). If it's loose or broken, starting the vehicle may be impossible until you tighten or replace it.
- Look at your gas gauge. Is it registering any fuel whatsoever?
- Is the vehicle equipped with any special antitheft mechanism that might prevent it from starting unless you take special steps? Your owner's manual should detail this.

About Your Dashboard Warning Lights

Not all dashboard warning lights are created equal. As a rule of thumb, expect to see all the lights (see figure 8-14) turn on briefly when you start the car. If none of them light when you start the vehicle, suspect a dead battery.

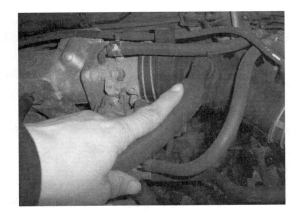

Fig. 8-13: Look beneath the hood for loose wires or hoses.

Fig. 8-14: It's normal to see all the dashboard warning lights display when you first start the vehicle and for 10 to 15 seconds afterward. Glance back at the dashboard to make certain none of the lights are still lit. Consult your manual to see what it says about the normal status of dashboard lights.

The worst thing you can do with these lights is to ignore them. They are there for a reason, either to alert you to a specific issue or to remind you to perform maintenance. Different manufacturers and various makes and models have their own abbreviations and warning light types. Your owner's manual is the best resource to determine what each light does and what it means when it comes on—or fails to do so when it should.

Some of these lights act as general warning signals to remind you of maintenance needs, such as the Check Engine light. A battery light may display when the vehicle senses the charge level is low or battery connections are loose. Others, like the oil light, often do not come on until the vehicle is in rather serious shape, such as when the oil level is dangerously low.

You should also check your owner's manual to determine how to fix burned-out dashboard lights; often this simply means replacing a small fuse located in a box under the hood or below the steering column.

WHAT DOES "FLOODING THE ENGINE" MEAN?

While most owner's manuals today do not recommend this, it is normal behavior for many drivers to depress the accelerator when starting their cars to send fuel into the system. What is not normal is to repeatedly depress or hold the accelerator down. Doing this sends far more fuel into the system than is needed to properly start the vehicle and the result is what is known as a flooded engine, although it is actually the carburetor that becomes flooded. Once you do this, you've created a whole new problem.

Time is usually the best cure for a flooded engine. Open the hood of the vehicle and wait for a few minutes before you try to start the vehicle again, this time being very careful about how much fuel you demand.

In extreme cases, you may have to open the carburetor—much as you did in replacing the air filter in chapter 6—and use an ether-based spray or WD-40 to try to dry up some of the excess fuel before you can start the car. Bear in mind, too, that ether-based sprays and WD-40 are highly flammable. Do not smoke or have the car running when you use them.

WARNING: An engine that easily floods may be a sign of a carburetor that needs adjustment. If you find yourself encountering a flooded engine frequently, schedule an appointment at your local garage to have this checked.

When the Ignition Key Doesn't Turn

The very first thing to do here is to make certain that you're using the correct key and that you have it firmly inserted. If the key is not seated properly, it will not turn as it should. Next, be sure that nothing, like a doodad or another key on your key chain, is obstructing the key's movement.

Now remove the key and inspect it as shown in figure 8-15. Does the key have a broken tooth or other damage? If so, locate your spare key and try that.

Also, some steering wheel columns and ignitions can lock in a specific way that will not allow you to turn the key. You may need to insert the key and try to move it to the On position and then manipulate the steering wheel to unlock it before you can turn the key to start the vehicle. Consult your owner's manual if you can't figure out how to do this.

Now look at your gear setting. As mentioned earlier, some vehicles must be in Park or Neutral to allow the ignition key to turn.

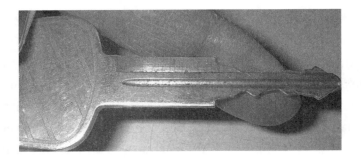

Fig. 8-15: Even minor damage to a key, such as a broken tooth or bending can render it unusable. Always have at least three keys for each lock and ignition, with one available to you at all times.

Next, check how your vehicle is parked. The ignition may lock, for example, if the tires are jammed up against a curb or turned in a certain way. If you think this may be the case in your situation, follow these steps:

1. Shift the vehicle into Park (neutral also should work for manual transmissions).
2. Make sure the parking and/or hand brake is set.
3. Yank the steering wheel in the opposite direction of how the tires are currently turned. If the steering wheel is locked, it should free up now.
4. Release the parking brake.
5. Shift the transmission into Neutral if it is not already there.
6. Turn the steering wheel again to make certain the movement is free.
7. Turn the ignition key.

What to Do If Your Vehicle Stalls and Won't Restart

Almost every vehicle stalls once in a great while. When it does it more frequently than that, it's time for some tender loving care in the form of good maintenance, such as performing a tune-up and inspecting the vehicle for problems such as loose connections, broken or loose belts, and fluid levels such as oil.

Where the problem of a stalled car becomes serious is when the vehicle refuses to start back up from the stall. Here, you will learn some of the items to check and tricks to try to get even the most recalcitrant vehicle back in operation.

Before you do anything else, turn off all accessories like unnecessary lights (your hazard lights should be turned on, however), the radio, and air conditioning. This reduces the chance you will drain the battery as you try to get the vehicle restarted. You should be careful how many times you try to turn over the engine because you can quickly end up with a battery too drained to operate, in which case you need to jump-start the vehicle (see chapter 6).

Also, if you noticed before the vehicle stalled that the temperature gauge was above normal range, you may want to let the vehicle cool down before you try again. Reread the section in this chapter on overheating to learn what to do.

If you've flooded the engine (or more appropriately, the carburetor), you need to let the vehicle sit for at least a few minutes to let the fuel level return to normal. Then try to restart the vehicle.

Consult your gas gauge. If the needle shows at or near empty, you've got to get some fuel into the vehicle or you won't go anywhere.

Check the dashboard lights with the ignition key set to On. After the initial lighting, are any still lit? This may provide a clue about the problem.

Next, open the hood and begin to inspect hoses and connections, especially the battery. Be careful about touching anything because the components are apt to still be quite hot. (Try to locate a rag to protect your hand.) Verify that the oil level isn't low.

Once the vehicle cools a bit more, you may want to check the distributor cap and the points to make certain everything is secure and you can see no damage. If you do spot damage, it's time to call the tow truck. If you're at home when this happens, you may want to remove one or more spark plugs (see chapter 6 on tune-ups) to see if these are particularly dirty; clean them with a rag before you return them to the cylinders and reconnect the wires running between the plug(s) and the distributor cap.

If it's a very wet day, your plugs and points may have become sodden and thus are not working. Refer to the section, "Steps to Take to Troubleshoot" earlier in this chapter to learn what you can do to dry them so the vehicle can be started.

If you have a car with a manual transmission, you may want to try to start the car by having one or more people push you, as described in chapter 7. But follow the precautions noted in that chapter, since this procedure can be dangerous.

If you have a vehicle with an automatic transmission, here is one more thing you can check if your vehicle starts but refuses to shift automatically into gear.

Locate your vehicle fuse box. Then, after you consult your owner's manual, see if you can determine which fuse controls the apply brake function on your vehicle. (Some fuse boxes also have a tiny but helpful diagram to show you which fuse corresponds to what function.) If this fuse blows, the car or truck will not move because it mistakenly believes the brake is engaged.

When you aren't sure if a fuse is blown—sometimes this is obvious because of a slight discoloration at one end of the fuse—you may want to replace it anyway just to see if this resolves the problem. Investing in a set of spare fuses for your vehicle is never a bad idea and often costs less than filling up a car with gas.

Coping with Poor Fuel/Oil Consumption

Statistics tell us that a poorly maintained vehicle can consume almost twice as much fuel and oil as a vehicle that has been properly maintained. This is one of the reasons regular maintenance has been discussed again and again in this book. Even if you feel you cannot afford the time or money for maintenance, you have to appreciate that you will end up spending as much or more for repairs and increased operating costs for a poorly maintained vehicle.

Thus, when you notice that your vehicle is consuming more fuel and/or oil than usual, you must ask yourself these questions:

1. When was the last time you performed a tune-up on your vehicle?
2. How long ago was your most recent oil change?
3. Are you carrying around excessive weight? Even 100 or 200 extra pounds of material in your trunk or cargo seat can drag down fuel efficiency.
4. How are your tires? Uneven or balding tires along with poor wheel alignment can degrade fuel efficiency.
5. Do you leave your vehicle idling for prolonged periods of time? This can be a serious waste of gas, not to mention adding to poor air quality from pollution.
6. Is most of your driving short hops? If so, you may want to step up maintenance because your vehicle isn't getting a chance to operate at its greatest efficiency.

If the answers to these questions point to lax maintenance, your best remedy is to schedule a weekend in which you perform an inspection, a tune-up, an oil change, and—if it's the right time of year—a radiator flush and water/coolant replacement. If your tires are worn or the alignment is off, make an appointment to have a realignment done and the tires rotated and/or replaced.

ARE YOU STILL BUYING PREMIUM GAS?

Every day, Americans shell out their hard-earned cash to pay the substantial price difference (sometimes 10 cents per gallon or more) between regular unleaded and premium. They do so assuming that somehow, their vehicles will run better and/or get better mileage by using premium.

Unfortunately, however, the vast majority of vehicles do not benefit from the differences between regular and premium. In fact, only extremely high-performance vehicles, like some sports cars, will respond to the specific properties of premium gas.

If you're one of the folks buying premium in a vain attempt to rev your Toyota Tercel or Ford Taurus, most experts recommend you just buy regular. The money will be better spent on performing the routine maintenance activities and repairs that can have a much greater impact on the overall performance and longevity of your vehicle.

Also, you might try getting your gas from a different station located in a different area. For instance, if you usually purchase fuel from a station located in a flood plain, try a station that isn't. You also may want to vary the brand of gas you get to see if one brand—for whatever reason—does better for you than another.

Use a notebook to keep track of your fill-ups and mileage. It could be that you are trying to estimate your average mileage based on imperfect calculations.

One final note: If your consumption of fuel or oil changes dramatically over a short period of time, you may want to use suggestions from earlier chapters to check for possible leaks. A neighbor of mine recently completed his first oil change on a new vehicle and noticed that suddenly, he was using more than a quart of oil per week. The problem turned out to be that he did not install his oil filter correctly and was losing oil from the vehicle.

9 KNOWING WHEN TO TAKE IT TO THE PROS

◆ What to do when you're stumped

◆ How to proceed when your efforts aren't resolving the issue

◆ Looking again at your vehicle warranty

◆ Finding and consulting a professional

◆ Requesting an estimate

◆ Making decisions about how to proceed

Throughout this book, you've learned a great deal about ways you can maintain your vehicle to prevent problems, identify issues even before they begin to affect your ability to drive your car, truck, or SUV, and fix many of the more common things that can go wrong, from a dead battery to a failing fan belt.

But it's important to appreciate that while you can be far more capable and responsible for your vehicle than you probably once thought, there are going to be some limits to what you can do on your own. This isn't conceding defeat but accepting situations where you need to call in the pros.

After all, if you realize you're not feeling so well, you can change your diet, increase your exercise, and generally attempt to make improvements to your lifestyle such as getting enough sleep. But if your health is still rocky after you make those changes, you probably wouldn't want to perform a triple bypass on yourself, right? Instead, you might first visit your family doctor, who might then refer you to a specialist. In this type of situation, it would be easy to understand that you've done what you can but it's time for the experts to take a look.

This same approach is smart for dealing with thornier vehicle issues as well. Sometimes the problems you face aren't something you absolutely could not fix on your own, but experts might be able to take care of them in a fraction of the time because they have the tools and parts readily available. They are also likely to have far more experience, a factor that can really help.

For some of you, however, the prospect of calling in a pro is not pleasant. Perhaps you decided to attempt your own maintenance and repairs because you had an experience where a problem never got fixed adequately or you felt someone ripped you off.

Yet there are certain repairs, especially those that require pulling an engine out of the car, that require a vehicle lift, or that otherwise call for special expertise or equipment, that are better left in the hands of the pros. This chapter is designed to help you not only identify which symptoms and situations warrant professional intervention but also how to get through the process like a savvy consumer.

Even if you opt to go to a pro for assistance, you can still exercise the same control you've exerted in doing smaller fixes and maintenance. Keep reading to find out how.

KNOWING WHAT A PRO SHOULD HANDLE

Once you commit to the idea of trying to be more hands-on about your vehicle's health, it can be difficult to change gears, so to speak, and decide to consult with or turn your vehicle over to a professional. But you should understand that you are not conceding defeat but being realistic about the value of your time.

So what are the kinds of jobs that you really should send to a professional mechanic for analysis and repair? Here are some examples:

- When you're stumped about how to proceed
- When you do not have the equipment required to do the job
- When you've tried unsuccessfully to make a repair
- When you may violate the terms of your warranty by proceeding with a repair on your own (see figure 9-1)

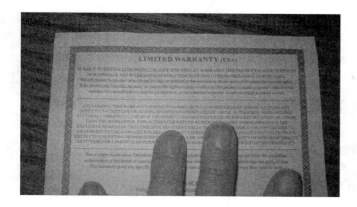

Fig. 9-1: Some automobile warranties are written more by lawyers than by normal mortals or knowledgeable mechanics. You may have to call the warranty company to make sense of some of your warranty's provisions.

- When a total system—like the fuel, brakes, exhaust, or transmission—may need analysis and overhaul and you do not feel comfortable handling this on your own
- When you cannot find enough information about what may need to be done to proceed with the repair yourself

RECHECK YOUR WARRANTY

If your vehicle is under warranty, it's especially important that you follow the advice in chapter 1 to read through your warranty. You need to understand what it covers and what actions it specifically precludes. Check also what it says about who can perform repairs (see figure 9-1). Some warranties limit your repair choices to the dealership where you bought the vehicle; others allow you to take the vehicle to any service shop that is approved by the car manufacturer.

Not everyone makes full use of his or her vehicle warranty. You may have already taken actions in other repairs that the issuer of the warranty could deem a violation. You also may have had bad experiences getting repairs done through your dealership or authorized service center. What you thought would be a no-cost repair may have ended with you paying a huge repair bill.

The deciding factors may be cost and convenience. It may be worth the extra trouble, including the distance you may need to travel, to take the vehicle to an authorized shop (sometimes listed as such in the yellow pages), especially if the repair will be covered at little or no cost to you. But if you're near the end of the warranty period and you think you can get the problem fixed better at a local shop rather than one located 30 or 50 miles away, it may be better to go with the local shop.

COVERING ALL BASES

Jennie is a successful businesswoman who has been doing many of her own vehicle repairs and maintenance since she was a poor college student. Like many people, she depends on her vehicles to operate reliably. She often has to travel large distances, so she needs dependable wheels.

She reports that she was burned several times when she brought her almost-new vehicles back to the dealership to get repairs that should have been covered under the warranty. She says the dealer often failed to fix her vehicles' problems, forcing her to pay for work out of her own pocket. So Jennie found two garages in her area that do a great job of handling problems with her car and SUV that are beyond her ability to fix. These garages have a much better track record with repairs than her dealership or other authorized service centers have had.

For a few years, she tried to force the manufacturers to cover under warranty those repairs she had done at the nonauthorized garages when the authorized venues did not help. She eventually devised a game plan that she says works well for her. When she has a repair she can't handle herself, she takes the vehicle in to one of the local garages she trusts to do an analysis of what needs to be done. She listens and takes notes. Then, armed with their report, she schedules an appointment with her dealership. When she brings the vehicle in, she sits down with the service manager to explain exactly what her garage tells her is wrong, and then points out the areas in the warranty document that prove this work should be covered.

Since she's been doing this, she reports she is getting much better service from the dealership. By going in armed with actual information, rather than telling them, "It makes this funny noise when I turn corners," she puts the dealership on notice that she is not going to accept less than a full repair. By doing this, she becomes an intelligent consumer who can say, "No, that's not correct," when the dealership tries to get away with making an inadequate repair attempt.

In the few instances where the dealership or other authorized service center still hasn't fixed the problem, she documents everything, insisting that the service manager write everything that was done on her repair slip, then takes the vehicle to one of the local garages. She then sends the bill for the work done by a nonauthorized garage to the warranty provider and demands that the bill be paid. About 80 percent of the time, she reports, the bill is paid, but only because she has all the documentation and a record of trying to get the repairs done the authorized way.

Jennie also subscribes to one of the notification services discussed in appendix A to alert her when there is a recall or a specific problem found with some part of her car. This has saved her big money, she says, on a defective catalytic converter and a long-standing problem with brakes that seemed to get "squishy" very soon after every repair. She reports that it has been easier to get the recall information directly from the Web site than by calling the dealership, which often claims to know nothing about recall issues that the subscription service has identified.

TRY TO GET A SENSE OF THE COST

Obviously, an estimate can be an important indication of what it will cost to repair the vehicle. But all too often, the actual costs can seem uncertain. If so, you need to ask questions and find out the specifics before you agree to have any work done (figure 9-2).

Also, consider getting an estimate from two or three different garages. Ask the garages to be as detailed as possible in their written estimates so you can compare them easily.

Understand that the lowest estimate may not provide you with the best results. For example, one garage may not include as much work in the estimate, which makes the price lower, while another garage might promise a much more comprehensive repair.

Also weigh what you may know of the reputation of a specific garage or its mechanics with the price of the work in making your decision.

There are always going to be times when an estimate suggested the price might come in around $100 and the final bill totals up to $150 or more. Only once a mechanic begins his or her work can an adequate assessment be made. Just ask for an explanation for the price difference. If something doesn't seem quite right, ask questions. Some states have specific laws regarding how much the final cost can exceed the estimate if you have not previously agreed to a change. The secretary of state's office for your state or resources available at your local library can help you find what the exact rules are regarding automotive estimates in your area.

FIND A PROFESSIONAL MECHANIC

Finding a highly professional and experienced mechanic can be a challenge. Obviously, one place to start is the yellow pages of your local phone directory. Many Web search engines like

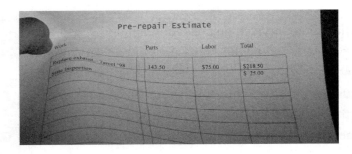

Fig. 9-2: Examine your estimate before you leave the garage. Ask the service manager or mechanic to spell out, in writing, any necessary details.

Yahoo and Google now have the capability to search for specific services in your local area, such as vehicle repair garages.

You can also use online resources like those listed in appendix A to help you find auto repair shops in your area. Some of these sites include Web-based message boards, such as www.jonko.com/auto_repair_forums, where you can leave questions and comments. There are also sites like Mechanic Review, available at www.mechanic-review.com, that allow you to search for well-rated professionals in your area. Also check to see if your community or county has its own Web site. You may be able to leave a question on such a site asking for a referral to a great garage or mechanic.

There are some other commonsense ways to find a good garage or mechanic, including asking friends, family members, neighbors, and coworkers for a recommendation; asking your local auto parts store to direct you to a good mechanic for your make and model of vehicle; and contacting your local Chamber of Commerce office.

REQUEST AN ESTIMATE

Have you ever had the experience of going into a garage and asking them to check your vehicle and prepare a detailed estimate of what needs to be done, only to arrive back at pickup time to be handed a bill for work they went ahead and did without your approval? Most of us have. The problem seems to be that garages don't usually make their profit on preparing estimates and analysis. Instead, they make their living through labor costs and the markup on parts.

Yet, as consumers, we also may have to take some responsibility for a breakdown in communications over vehicle repairs. Too often, we don't feel comfortable enough with the terminology of car repairs to be clear about what we want. We need to make certain that the person behind the service counter understands exactly what we are asking for.

Be prepared to ask questions, like:

- How much will the estimate cost? Some places advertise free estimates, only to present you with a bill once they complete the estimate. They then explain that the estimate is free only if they do the exact repairs they recommend. But a free estimate should be free. Be sure of what you're getting into before you agree to anything.
- What type of work will the garage do in performing the estimate? Just a glance at the vehicle may not tell the mechanic anything. While you can't expect him or her to take the vehicle apart to diagnose a problem, you should expect a reasonable job of testing and analysis. The shorter the time spent looking at the vehicle, the less value the estimate may have.
- What experience does the garage or the specific mechanic who will work on your vehicle have with your vehicle type? Not every mechanic knows every type of vehicle. A mechanic who is great at fixing family sedans may not be so hot on special repairs for a foreign-made SUV. Ask if there is another mechanic available who does know your make and model of vehicle so time is not wasted.
- Is the garage an authorized service center for your vehicle? This matters in terms of your warranty.
- What guarantee or warranty does the garage give on its work? Establish this before you have a garage or mechanic do any work and, if possible, get it in writing. This can help you avoid a situation where you have to pay for the same work to be redone once or twice because a repair was not made correctly the first time. Also, if parts need to be replaced, try to determine if these parts have a warranty and also get this in writing. If the same part needs to be replaced again during the warranty period, you should not have to pay for the part again.
- When can they do the work if you want to go ahead? While you may not want to schedule the repair immediately—for example, you may want to get other estimates—you should ask how soon the garage can go ahead and perform the repairs. Also try to get a sense for how long the work is expected to take. This is necessary because you may have

Savvy Tip

Read any paperwork you get from a garage—or just about anywhere else, for that matter—carefully. The back of the sheet, for example, may contain a fair amount of fine print that needs perusal. But the front of the sheet may specify certain things as well, such as the length of the guarantee or warranty on the work and special clauses you should note.

to make other arrangements like having someone pick you up for work or getting a rental car during the time the vehicle is being serviced. Sometimes a garage can lend you a vehicle for a nominal fee.

Beware of any garage that puts up serious resistance to giving you a complete estimate in writing. If all it is willing to do is to jot two or three things down on a slip, that may not give you enough to go on. While the garage may be great and it's just a matter of people who aren't good at filling out forms, you want a document you can fall back on if the results don't meet your expectations.

MAKE THE SCOPE CLEAR

Assume nothing. If you're leaving your vehicle off for an estimate, you should be clear that you do not want the mechanic to start the actual repair until someone contacts you to tell you what is wrong, what needs to be done, and how much the repair may cost.

If you want them to start the repair, specify any conditions you want to place on the work. For example, "If you find something else that needs to be fixed, please contact me before you proceed," or "Right now, I don't want to spend more than the $200 or so you've estimated, so contact me if you see a need to go further." This can reduce the chance your under-$100 repair blossoms into an $800 repair without your authorization.

Make certain, too, that whoever you leave the keys with writes down your specifics, including any limitations on the work as well as your contact information. While your auto is the only thing you're concerned about, understand that the garage may be dealing with a dozen or more other vehicles that day. What you tell someone behind the counter at 7:30 a.m. may be forgotten by 9 a.m. or noon if you don't make sure he or she recorded the details.

The flip side of the person who doesn't speak up is the type who arrives at the garage ready to do battle against mechanics who are trying to rip him or her off. While it's good to be attentive

Savvy Tip

All too often, we plan what we'll say to the mechanic or garage only to arrive and get tongue-tied. Jot yourself a note if you need to do so, but make your thoughts clear to the person responsible for your vehicle. A contract of any kind requires a meeting of the minds of all parties concerned; if you do not communicate your needs, who will?

to detail and to expect that what you pay for is actually done, you probably won't serve yourself well if you go in loaded for bear.

ASK TO SEE THE PARTS REMOVED AND THE WORK DONE

Here's a nasty situation that has been seen time and again with less-than-honorable garages: they tell you they've replaced one or three different parts on your car but you find out later on—perhaps because you continue to have problems and take the vehicle to yet another garage—that the garage never replaced those parts at all.

One way to try to put a garage on notice that you want proof is to ask—before the work is begun—to see the actual parts removed by the time you have to settle up the bill. Some people even go so far as to request to see both the replacement parts and the parts removed. While a questionable garage could still get one over on you, you may make it more difficult for them to do so if you indicate you want proof.

Also ask the service manager or mechanic to go over the vehicle with you to show you exactly what was done. Don't be afraid to ask questions. I've learned how to do a few repairs myself from sessions where a mechanic told me what he or she did to fix a problem. Some are willing to take the time to educate you. This kind of information session also helps you understand what was wrong and to explain the situation to the next mechanic if the problem recurs.

What do you do if the mechanic who worked on your vehicle isn't there when you pick up the vehicle and pay the bill? If no one else there did work on it, ask when the mechanic will be back and try to schedule a time—as soon as possible—to come back in to ask your questions.

COPING WITH SUBPAR RESULTS

Even if you follow all the recommendations offered in this chapter and the other resources provided in this book, it's possible that you may go through the process of having a professional repair your vehicle only to find the results aren't great. So what do you do?

The first thing you should do is contact the place where you had the repair done and explain the situation to them. Don't let more than a few days pass, however, because you want the repairs fresh in their minds and you don't want to give them the chance to argue that your misuse of the vehicle since you picked it up caused the current problem.

It's also important that you be patient and reasonable. If the garage suggested a larger repair and you went with a very minimal one against their recommendation, it's possible that the larger repair would have solved the problem. It's also possible that the problem you have now is a new one, or affects a different part of the car than you had fixed.

If the mechanic throws up his or her hands and says there is nothing more that can be done, you have to weigh your options. If you believe the garage or mechanic acted in bad faith and you have documented proof that they agreed to satisfy the problem, you may be able to seek a legal remedy.

But legal recourse takes time and you need the vehicle now. So you may want to consider having another garage do the work and document any problem they see with the first garage's work. Then you can try to get the first garage to pick up the costs of your subsequent repair by suing in small claims court or seeking help through your local Better Business Bureau.

Is the garage where you had the work done part of a larger company? If so, you may want to contact the parent company.

If you had the repair done by a dealership or an authorized service center, only to find that garage now unwilling to properly correct the problem, you have a few options. You can go to the head of the dealership and tell that person you won't buy another vehicle there if you're going to get poor service.

If you get little response from the dealership or service center, you may want to write or call the main headquarters of the car manufacturer and explain the situation. While this usually doesn't provide an immediate fix, it may get the ball rolling to get you the repairs you've already paid for.

CONGRATULATIONS!

In nine chapters, you have covered a great deal of ground.

Hopefully, you now feel far more empowered to treat the part of your vehicle under the hood as no longer a mystery but a place where you can take real, commonsense steps to investigate, troubleshoot, and repair a host of issues that crop up on just about every vehicle at one time or another. You've also learned powerful tips for finding a good mechanic and dealing with him or her by asking intelligent questions and understanding the answers.

Equally important, you now know about the all-important maintenance that can keep your car, truck, SUV, or minivan from breaking down in the first place. Changing oil, for example, is a job no one loves to do, but you can prolong the great life of your vehicle by years if you do it on schedule.

Do yourself a favor and keep this book handy. Refer to it from time to time, even when your vehicle is running well. The maintenance steps alone can keep you from a nasty breakdown on a long stretch of road where few other cars come by and your cell phone can't get service. And, of course, such breakdowns always occur at the worst times, such as on the coldest night of winter and the most miserably simmering day of summer. Breakdowns also love to happen when you're short on cash and your credit cards are maxed out.

Think about it: you won't just save your vehicle. You'll save your life and sanity. That's never a bad deal.

Happy driving!

APPENDIX: CAR REPAIR AND MAINTENANCE RESOURCES ONLINE

- ◆ Why going online for additional help makes sense
- ◆ What you can find online
- ◆ How to locate more Web resources
- ◆ A look at some helpful sites

One of the most helpful tools for getting assistance with your vehicle's repair and maintenance needs, beyond those covered in this book, is your home computer and your Internet connection.

WHAT'S AVAILABLE ONLINE TO HELP YOU

How-to assistance has always been a popular topic online. With the emergence of the World Wide Web in the early to mid-1990s, along with the development of technology that allowed mere mortals to set up their own Web sites and then add digital photos, audio, and even movies to those sites, millions of people have gone online not just to look for assistance but also to share their own wisdom and experiences. From rank amateurs to pros with decades of on-the-job know-how, people are sharing online.

Today, there's quite a do-it-yourself boom going on. Whether you're looking for help with installing a toilet, creating a really sophisticated wireless home network, or learning how to tune your car engine, you can find it online.

Do you enjoy listening to the weekly public radio show Car Talk? That show's hosts have been on the Web (visit www.cartalk.com) for about a decade. Other vehicle-focused radio and TV programs have Web sites as well.

Yet that's hardly all. On the Web, you can find:

- general and specific articles on repair and maintenance;
- step-by-step tutorials that show you different ways you can do various things, including both simple and complex repairs and routine maintenance;
- explanations of how different systems within your car (fuel, brakes, exhaust, heating and cooling, transmission, and more) work and the various parts involved;
- where to obtain parts, tools, and books relating to your type of vehicle(s);
- CDs and videos to purchase that help you perform more advanced repairs;
- what to look for before you take your vehicle to a professional for evaluation;
- what questions to ask of your professional once you do take the vehicle in;
- auto stores and repair centers in your area, along with general prices for various services, including lube jobs, brakes, transmission, and exhaust system replacement; and
- subscription services where you can access fairly specific information about your vehicle.

Many of the resources provided here are free or, at least, offer some free areas where you can read articles, find prices, or view some basic tutorials. Where there are fees involved, these are noted in this appendix.

Understand too that this section is just a start. Resources on the Internet change all the time; existing sites become unavailable or change substantially, while new ones go online frequently. That's why you'll get a short primer on finding resources yourself, above and beyond those listed here.

There's an old saying about only believing some of what you read and less than half of what you see. This rule applies to Web sites as well. It's not all that unusual to find conflicting information. One site tells you to use this type of oil while another says you should use another. You'll also occasionally find outright mistakes. When in doubt, it's usually better to do additional research and try to find a consensus of opinion rather than just flipping a coin to guess what's right.

SOME RECOMMENDED PLACES TO START

To get you started with the assistance and resources you can find online, I've done some of the footwork for you. Then, in the next section, I'll give you some hints about how you can find more, either for your specific vehicle make and model or for diagnosis and repairs that go beyond the scope of this book.

As you read, remember what I mentioned before: sites change all the time; they may become super sites with lots more goodies, including articles and help, or they may get bought up by a commercial-only site whose only purpose is selling you something. Others may get neglected and/or abandoned or close up shop altogether. So don't be surprised if the sites you see here look quite different by the time you visit.

10W40.com

Named for the ever-popular grade of motor oil, the site 10W40.com, pictured in figure A-1, offers what it calls the ultimate auto repair directory. Use its free online database to search for auto repair articles, parts, and supplies from across the Web. This makes it very much like a specialized search engine devoted to the topic of keeping your vehicles healthy.

Alldata.com/products/diy or alldatadiy.com

ALLDATA (see figure A-2) is an example of a subscription service. In this case, you subscribe to information about each of the vehicles you have so you can access very specific information

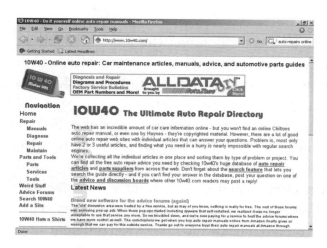

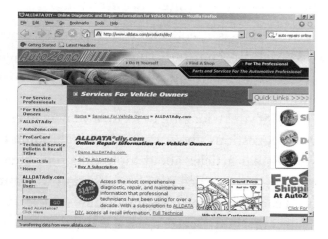

Fig. A-1: 10W40.com (www.10w40.com) features a database where you can locate articles, tutorials, and how-to features, along with information about parts and supplies gleaned from other vehicle repair sites across the country.

Fig. A-2: ALLDATA.com (www.ALLDATA.com/products/diy), an AutoZone company, is a subscription service that puts some of the details only the pros usually have right at your fingertips.

on repairs, parts, and maintenance for each. For $24.95 per year for your first vehicle and $14.95 for each additional car, you get:

- factory recall and technical service bulletins (often called just TSBs);
- diagnostic and repair procedures geared toward specific makes and models (complete with full illustrations);
- manufacturer's part numbers for easier locating and ordering;
- component locations and diagrams so you can find where a part is located and what else it connects to; and
- factory maintenance schedules and recommendations (although this is usually available in your owner's manual).

AutoEducation.com

Just as its name suggests, AutoEducation.com exists to help you learn more about your vehicle(s). Different pages on AutoEducation.com discuss different systems in your car, truck, or SUV ranging from the electrical system to cooling and heating to brakes and exhaust. Other links on the site point you to free do-it-yourself auto repair articles as well as places to buy repair manuals for specific vehicle makes and models. There is no charge for viewing the content here.

Auto Repair and Maintenance Web Ring

A Web ring is a collection of Web sites devoted to a specific topic; this one, available at www.webring.com/hub?ring=autorepairandmaintenance, is just up your repair alley, so to speak. Here you'll find sites run by professionals as well as amateur car enthusiasts offering a little bit of everything, from auto repair and maintenance to advice on restoring a classic model (useful if you're looking to fix up a vehicle to resell it at top dollar) and other commonsense tips and suggestions about cars in general. Some recommend specific products while others give you regular articles about topics like replacing your brakes, improving your gas mileage, and dealing with service professionals and warranties. Others offer tips on what to look for in a used car or in purchasing an all-new vehicle. Each site features links to all the other sites in the Web ring—in this case, there are 100 or more—so you can quickly move between different sites until you find what you want.

AutoZone.com

This site offers a couple of superbly helpful features. One is free access to online vehicle repair guides from models dating from 1950 to 2000. To use this:

1. Click the Vehicle Repair Guides link from the main page on AutoZone.com (figure A-3).
2. Pick your vehicle year.
3. Choose from one of the basic vehicle makes and models listed (not all are there, but enough so that many should be able to get some assistance).
4. Select the model that most closely matches yours (see figure A-4)
5. Pick the topic or system you want to review.

Look at figure A-5 and you see that I've found some basic information on the brake system on my old but still reliable workhorse of a Suzuki Sidekick 4x4. Links at the right let me explore additional topics, or I could go back and choose a different system in the car to learn about. The second feature you may find useful is also available from AutoZone's home page: the Find a Shop feature. There, you can search for auto repair shops in your area by plugging in your zip code. You can specify what type of service or repair you're looking for and get contact information for each garage.

ChiltonsOnline.com

Remember in chapter 1 where you learned about special auto repair books published for different makes and models of cars? Chilton guides, published by Thomson Delmar Learning, are

Fig. A-3: AutoZone.com (www.autozone.com) has a number of helpful features, including the ability to look up repair specifics and general information as well as find a shop for repairs.

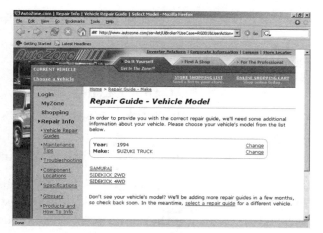

Fig. A-4: Check AutoZone's repair manual list to see if you can find your make and model so you can explore the manual online, without the extra cost of getting a separate reference book. You can always print out pages, if needed.

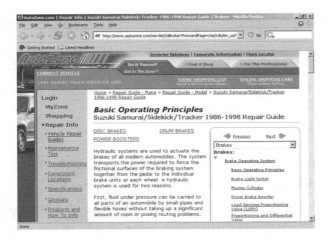

Fig. A-5: Using AutoZone's online repair manual, you can research different systems, as well as basic repairs and maintenance, for your make and model of vehicle.

Fig. A-6: Chilton Diagnostics (www.chiltonsonline .com) is a subscription-only service allowing both professional technicians and serious auto enthusiasts to locate detailed specifications about their vehicles.

one of the most popular of these and here you can browse through their complete selection. You may also want to check out www.chiltondiagnostics.com, shown in figure A-6, a subscription service targeted at professional car technicians. As part of this service, you can track down those computer error codes discussed in the first few chapters of this book.

FactoryAutoManuals.com

Unlike the Chilton and Haynes sites, which only hawk their own repair manuals, FactoryAutoManuals.com lets you try to track down any auto manual ever produced for both foreign and domestic vehicles. Their products include both original documentation for your vehicle as well as third party–published manuals like some of the guides mentioned elsewhere in this book. Even if you're not in the market to buy one of these manuals new, you can use this site as a reference to find out if any published material exists for your vehicle and then try to locate it through another source, such as a used book store.

Haynes

Haynes is the online home of the Haynes auto repair guides discussed first in chapter 1. They're based in England; you can find them at www.haynes.co.uk. Non-pros tend to like the Haynes books because they're fairly comprehensive and contain a slew of detailed diagrams as well as

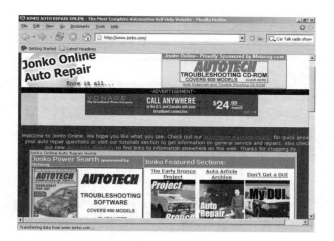

Fig. A-7: Jonko.com (www.jonko.com) features some easy-to-follow instructions on performing both common and not-so-common repairs and routine maintenance procedures.

Fig. A-8: Browse through the articles at *Popular Mechanics* magazine's Web site (www.popularm echanics.com/automotive) and locate both current and past articles related to auto repair and maintenance.

step-by-step instructions for performing common repairs and parts replacements. We once used their Suzuki Samurai guide to do a complicated engine repair even though neither of us is an expert technician in anything other than PC repair. Also, as you find with Chilton's guides and others, you aren't limited just to print books (although these books are easy to carry with you out to the garage or driveway). Material is also available on CDs and DVDs that can be played on your home TV setup or through your personal computer.

Jonko.com

Looking for step-by-step tutorials along with vehicle repair tips and tricks? Try Jonko.com (see figure A-7), which has both. There are also Web-based forms to help you locate special car repair and diagnostic software that can work far more interactively than a print book in helping you identify the problems' underlying symptoms as well as the components in your vehicle and its many systems. Extras here that you can't get at every site include message boards where you can leave questions, find answers, and read about problems people are discussing.

Popular Mechanics

You no doubt know the magazine is written for the consumer rather than the professional audience. But not only does this magazine have an online presence, it includes a whole section on do-it-yourself auto repair and maintenance, available at www.popularmechanics.com/automotive (see figure A-8).

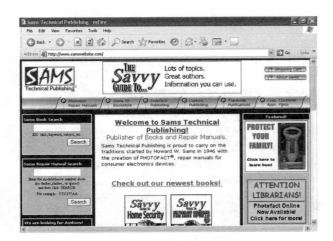

Fig. A-9: *Road and Travel* magazine's Car Care center (www.roadandtravel.com/carcare) features special areas for women and amateur mechanics that avoid all the techie terminology so you can understand what you need to do.

Fig. A-10: Expand the value of your Sams technical books through the Sams Technical Publishing Web site (www.samswebsite.com), which has lots of great reference material on a host of topics and links to other Sams titles.

Road and Travel Magazine's Car Care

Published by the same folks who bring you *Road and Travel* magazine, their special car care section, available at www.roadandtravel.com/carcare, offers articles, tips, and more, including a special Women's Workshop (see figure A-9). While there are links to archived older material, you'll find fresh information posted just about every month.

Sams Technical Publishing

Sams Technical Publishing (www.samswebsite.com) is a publisher of savvy technical reference publications on a variety of topics, including auto repair. Additional information from their books can often be found online through the site, which acts as a 24/7 companion to the Sams texts you buy. (See figure A-10.)

TalkAboutAutos.com

This site's value is apparent in its name, as it features online discussions and specialty forums (see figure A-11) allowing you to learn a great deal about your make and model of vehicle. You can find links for parts and vehicle restoration, read new car model reviews, and even learn some of the tips and tricks for getting the best rate when you need a new car loan.

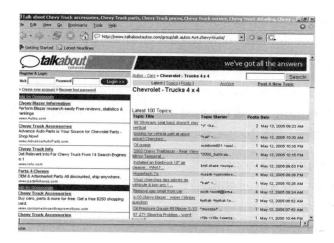

Fig. A-11: Choose the forum devoted to your make/model of vehicle from TalkAboutAutos' (www.talkaboutautos.com) list, which includes foreign models like Suzuki and Volvo.

TrustMyMechanic.com

While this site is geared to the promotion of a book by the same name, you'll also locate some very helpful free information about some of the most common automotive problems. Besides diagnosing and troubleshooting, articles here answer some frequently asked questions on car repair and maintenance, provide a before-you-buy used car checklist, and inform you about everything you need to know about the different grades of motor oil.

FINDING YOUR OWN WEB RESOURCES ON AUTO REPAIR AND MAINTENANCE

Don't be afraid to ask your friends, coworkers, family members, and, yes, even your local auto parts store clerks and mechanics for recommendations. More than one mechanic has pointed me to a great Web site where I either found very reasonable parts or accessories or learned a great deal about specific problems with my vehicle that mechanics usually don't have the time to explain.

If you live in an area that has a number of different chain auto parts, repair, and maintenance shops, it may be helpful to go to their sites for the location of their shops and local prices. Good examples are www.jiffylube.com and www.pepboys.com.

More and more Web sites let you make online appointments for your vehicle. However, just to be safe, I recommend you actually call the local shop or garage afterwards to verify your appointment.

You can use a Web search engine to help you locate additional online resources. There are a slew of different search engines and for best results you should check at least three or more. Some of the search engines I like to use include:

- Altavista at www.altavista.com
- Ask Jeeves at www.askjeeves.com
- Dogpile at www.dogpile.com
- Google at www.google.com
- Lycos at www.lycos.com
- Yahoo at www.yahoo.com

Use the Help section of each of these search engines to refine your search.

GLOSSARY

While you've likely picked up the meaning of many terms in this book through your reading, the day-to-day operation of your vehicle, and visits to professional garages, it helps to be sure you understand all the basics. Although this is not meant as a definitive guide—there are hundreds if not thousands of additional terms—this glossary lists some of the most common vehicle components and terms.

Remember, however, that if you have to take your vehicle to a garage and a mechanic uses a term you either don't know or aren't sure about, ask. Actually, it doesn't hurt to ask what is meant even if you think you understand; this reduces the likelihood that what you believe is 180 degrees from what the mechanic meant. When you pay for professional repairs, take advantage of the knowledge of the mechanic you're working with.

You should also know that there are additional resources online, besides those listed in the appendix, that provide definitions for hundreds and sometimes thousands of automotive terms. One that's particularly good is www.autoglossary.com.

Here's a final tip: if one dictionary defines a term in a way you don't understand, check the entry in one or more other auto repair glossaries. Sometimes, you can glean enough from multiple definitions to get a better picture of what the item or repair is.

air filter—A filter usually positioned over the carburetor to limit the amount of dust, dirt, and debris that can enter the carburetor.

air/fuel ratio—Refers to the balance required in a combustion engine to allow for proper burning of fuel by being sure there is sufficient—but not too much—oxygen in the mix.

air injection—One of the methods used to reduce the most harmful vehicle emissions by adding or injecting air into either the exhaust manifold or the catalytic converter.

air pump—Usually a belt-driven pump that produces and helps inject air to reduce harmful emissions in an air injection vehicle.

all-season tires—Tires that have been specifically engineered to provide increased traction on wet, icy, and snow-covered roads while still allowing for good handling on dry road surfaces.

alternator—A part on many vehicles that converts mechanical energy to electrical energy.

antifreeze—Also called "coolant," this is usually either ethylene glycol (green in color) or propylene glycol (usually red in color) that is used in the radiator to protect the vehicle from extremes of temperature. Never use straight antifreeze; there usually needs to be a 50-50 mix of antifreeze and water.

antilock braking system (ABS)—A type of brake that automatically measures wheel speed and makes immediate adjustments through hydraulic pressure applied to the brakes; it is designed to reduce the chance of the brakes locking or the vehicle going into a skid when the brakes are applied.

anti-smog device—One or more parts added to a vehicle exhaust system in states that require them; these are designed to reduce the level of certain emissions (see **auto emissions**) that contribute to smog.

auto emissions—Unwanted gases and related substances produced during the operation of a vehicle, usually including carbon monoxide, hydrocarbons, and oxides of nitrogen.

auto maintenance—A routine of regular care for a vehicle that includes checking and adjusting fluid levels, inspecting the vehicle for problems, replacing fouled fluids like oil and coolant, and taking other measures to prolong good vehicle performance and vehicle life.

automatic transmission fluid (ATF)—A red petroleum-based liquid used to cool, lubricate, and usually clean a vehicle equipped with an automatic transmission.

auxiliary shaft—Found in overhead cam engines, this is a separate shaft that operates support components like the distributor, fuel pump, oil pump, and sometimes the water pump.

axle—This is one of the central supporting structural parts of a vehicle; axles come off the center support running from the front to the rear of a vehicle and serve as crosspieces to which one or more wheels are directly attached or by which they are supported.

battery—A replaceable and rechargeable electromechanical device used to store and provide electrical power to start the vehicle and maintain certain electrical functions such as lights and radio.

battery jump—*See* **jump start.**

battery posts—Also called battery terminals, these are the two post-like structures on a battery to which cables from the vehicle are attached.

blown engine— An engine that has become severely damaged, usually through poor maintenance or abuse.

blown rod— A major engine problem where one or more of the rods within the cylinders has been irreparably damaged.

brake—The part of the vehicle responsible for slowing or stopping movement of the wheels; there are many different types of brakes and brake systems, including disc, drum, computer controlled, automatic, antilock, power, hydraulic, and electrical.

brake caliper—Part of a disc brake system that helps convert hydraulic pressure into mechanical force; usually includes the piston and brake pads.

brake drum—Part of the brake cylinder that moves with the wheels; brake shoes surround the drum.

brake pad—Usually refers to the brake lining, an abrasive material, much like a heavy grade sandpaper, that helps grab the wheel(s) to slow or stop a vehicle.

brake shoe—A curved or contoured part of the brake surrounding the brake drum that is pushed against the brake drum to slow or stop the wheel movement.

camshaft—A shaft within the engine that is controlled by the crankshaft.

carburetor—Part of a combustion engine whose job is to provide the delicate air-fuel mixture needed for proper operation.

catalytic converter—A part of the exhaust system whose primary responsibility is to neutralize certain compounds that would normally be expelled through the exhaust tailpipe.

choke—A component that helps control the flow of air to the carburetor, depending on the operating temperature of the vehicle; if the engine is cold, the choke assembly closes the aperture to reduce the air; when the engine is warm, the choke opens the aperture.

clutch—A mechanism on a manual-transmission vehicle, controlled by a foot pedal located at the far left of the pedal row, that helps prepare the engine to shift into a different gear. Without the proper engagement of the clutch during shifting, the gears can be stripped or damage can be done to the teeth that help set the gear, possibly making one or more gears inoperable.

coil or coil spring—A very strong component of the vehicle suspension that lets the vehicle move up and down in response to road conditions that might otherwise damage the body; this coil usually supports the vehicle's weight and helps it maintain its height and balance.

cooling system—The parts of a vehicle involved in the cooling of the engine to prevent overheating and engine failure.

crank—*See* **crankshaft**.

crankshaft—A revolving component usually located near the bottom of the engine.

cylinder—The round holes in an engine that accommodate the engine pistons as they move up and down as part of the vehicle operation. *See also* **wheel cylinder**.

cylinder block—The basic frame of the engine to which all or most parts of the engine are attached.

diagnostic trouble code—*See* **DTC**.

distributor—A component that directs electrical current to the spark plugs.

distributor cap—The cover for the distributor; if the distributor cap is damaged, replace it immediately.

DTC—Stands for diagnostic trouble code, a code generated by a computer-based vehicle to help identify a problem, such as low oil pressure, brake malfunction, cooling issues, etc.; a special device that connects to an outlet below the steering column allows the DTC to be read.

DTC code reader—A device that connects to an outlet inside the vehicle to read diagnostic codes generated by an onboard computer.

engine—The part of a vehicle that is responsible for the burning of fuel to produce power to operate the vehicle; there are many different types of engines but an internal combustion engine that burns gasoline remains the most common.

engine knock—The harsh compression sound that is heard when the air-fuel mixture ignites but burns too quickly; this should be checked to reduce the chance of damage to the engine.

exhaust system—Refers to the parts of the vehicle like the muffler, catalytic converter, and tailpipe involved with removing emissions from the vehicle.

fan belt—A drive belt that takes power from the crankshaft pulley and transfers it to other parts like the alternator and water pump.

flushing the radiator—Using water to clean out the radiator system to remove impurities and broken-down coolant, preparing the radiator for a fresh 50-50 coolant-water mixture.

frame—The core of the substructure of a vehicle, the frame supports not only the passenger compartment but also the engine, power train, and other parts of the vehicle body

freeplay—The amount of time between the depression of the brake pedal and the engagement of the brake.

front suspension—The part of the suspension system that supports the front end of the vehicle.

fuel injection—A system found on many vehicles that carefully controls the amount of fuel sprayed or injected into the engine.

gear—Typically, a transmission gear speed.

jump start—Restoring power to a depleted battery by connecting it through jumper cables to another working battery or to a special device that can be plugged into household current and then used to recharge the depleted battery.

knocking—*See* **engine knocking**.

magneto—An electrical device that delivers current to the spark plugs.

main body—The primary construction of the vehicle, which includes the body panels, underbody, roof, doors, dashboard, and deck lid.

manifold—Although there are many components of a vehicle with this name, it usually refers to a conduit responsible for moving the gas-air mixture into the engine or moving exhaust from the engine to the exhaust system.

master cylinder—The core of the brake system, this is where the brake fluid resides and where pressure is produced to slow or stop the wheels.

misfire—A condition in which the air-fuel mixture in the vehicle does not ignite properly.

muffler—An integral part of the exhaust system charged with reducing the overall noise of the car's operation.

odometer—The mechanical or electronic device in a vehicle that measures the total number of miles driven; in most parts of the country, it is illegal to manipulate the count on an odometer.

oil change—Part of regular car maintenance that involves draining used oil from the vehicle and replacing it with fresh oil as well as a fresh oil filter.

oil filter—A device that removes dirt and impurities before they can enter the engine.

oil viscosity—The overall thickness of different types of oil used in combustible engines.

piston—Although vehicles usually have more than one type of piston, this commonly refers to the component inside the engine cylinders that moves up and down.

plugs—*See* **spark plugs.**

points—Also called ignition points, these are located in the distributor body under the distributor cap where the rotor is located; as the rotor turns, it distributes the electrical charge from the battery to the ignition points as it contacts them one by one. The points are connected by ignition wires to the spark plugs, which ignite the engine.

primer—A special type of paint used to prep the vehicle surface for paint as well as to stop further development of rust on the body.

radiator—A core part of the automotive cooling system; fins and tubes found at the core of the radiator remove heat from the coolant to keep the engine running within normal temperature ranges.

radiator cap—A pressurized cap positioned at the top of the radiator.

radiator hose—A heat-resistant hose that runs between the radiator and the outer housing of the thermostat used to control vehicle temperature.

rear suspension—The part of the vehicle suspension system responsible for bearing the load and distribution for the rear half of the vehicle.

ring job—Repair or replacement of the rings that act like gaskets inside the cylinder to "wipe" excess oil from the pistons as they move up and down; blue smoke coming from the tailpipe can be a strong indicator of defective rings.

rust—The common term for oxidation of metal that results in an eating away of the metal.

shock absorber—Part of the vehicle suspension system, one of these is positioned at every wheel to try to limit the up-and-down and rolling motions of the vehicle and limit the damage to the vehicle caused by such motions.

snow tire—A type of tire designed with a special emphasis on the treads best suited to perform on ice and snow; many communities and states have laws about the removal of snow tires after a specific date at the end of cold weather.

spark plugs—Part of the ignition system, one of these sits at the top of each engine cylinder to help ignite the air/fuel mixture.

speedometer—A gauge that registers the rate of speed a vehicle travels; this may be shown on an LED display.

suspension—A system within a vehicle, usually computerized, that controls unusual movements to keep the vehicle balanced.

tail pipe—The last part of the exhaust system, this carries exhaust from the vehicle out to the rear, reducing overall temperature and preventing toxic fumes from building up inside the passenger compartment.

thermostat—Usually refers to the part of the cooling system that monitors the temperature of the engine and helps control the cooling system's response to extremes of temperature that could damage the engine.

timing belt—A belt that helps the crankshaft drive the camshaft(s).

timing chain—*See* **timing belt**.

timing light—A strobe light used to adjust the proper alignment of the timing belt.

tire rotation—The regular rearranging of tires on a vehicle to try to maintain even wear and extend tire life; the owner's manual usually specifies the recommended number of miles between tire rotations.

transmission—The part of a vehicle that controls the operation of the gears and adjustment of the engine.

tune-up—Part of essential vehicle maintenance, a tune-up usually involves replacing the spark plugs and air filter.

valve job—One of the more labor-intensive engine repairs, this is a process by which a cylinder head, including the valves, is reconditioned; the goal is to restore engine performance and reduce the amount of excessive oil consumption combined with oily smoke.

vehicle identification number (**VIN**)—The unique identifying number assigned to each new vehicle to help track the vehicle during its lifetime; this number is usually mounted in two, three, or more places, such as at the intersection of the dashboard and the windshield, the engine block, or the frame near one of the front doors.

wheel chocks—Anything placed in front of or behind the tires to prevent a vehicle from being able to roll.

wheel—The hub of an axle on which a tire is mounted.

wheel alignment—A usually computer-guided readjustment of tires to bring them in line with the normal operation of the vehicles; driving extensively in ice and snow or on bad roads can contribute to poor alignment, which can make it far more difficult to steer the vehicle because of the potential delay in wheel response.

wheel cylinder—A critical part involved in wheel and brake operation, the wheel cylinder sits on the backing plate of a drum brake assembly and converts the hydraulic pressure that comes from the master cylinder into mechanical energy to press against the brake shoe to slow or stop a wheel.

wheel cylinder piston—The part of the wheel cylinder that pushes against the brake drum.

wheel shimmy—A loose or wobbly sensation from a tire or wheel often caused by poor wheel alignment.

INDEX

ABOUT THE AUTHOR

Kate J. Chase is a freelance journalist and reference book author based in Marshfiled, Vermont. As a writer and journalist, she has occasionally found herself either short on money for car repairs or replacement or out in the middle of nowhere on assignment with a broken-down car—or both. Couple that with being a woman who's occasionally gotten some incredibly "creative" estimates from repair shops and you have someone who's learned how to do essential car repair and maintenance out of necessity. She brings to the topic the same savvy, intelligent "get control of your machine" approach Kate teaches her readers in her PC books.

Kate's work has included articles in the *New York Times* and many other newspapers and magazines. She's written hundreds of product reviews, help articles, and feature stories appearing online. She has also authored, contributed to, revised, or edited more than two dozen PC reference books including *Buying Rx Drugs Online* (Course Technology, 2005), *Norton All-in-One Desk Reference for Dummies* (Wiley, 2005), *PC Hardware and A+Handbook* (Microsoft Press, 2004), and *PC Disaster and Recovery* (Sybex, 2003).

PUBLISHING

SAMS Technical Publishing LLC